DESKTOP MANAGER
User's Manual

A File Management Utility for Xerox Ventura Publisher

Version 1.00

New Riders Publishing, Thousand Oaks, CA

DESKTOP MANAGER

User's Manual

Published By:

New Riders Publishing
P.O. Box 4846
Thousand Oaks, CA 91360
USA

Library of Congress Card Catalog Number: 88-61192

DESKTOP MANAGER
A File Management Utility for Xerox Ventura Publisher

ISBN: 0-934035-34-2

Warning And Disclaimer

Acknowledgments

The program's author would like to thank all of those who made this program possible.

Thanks to Jesse Berst for his constant support and input on the program's features. Without his involvement the program literally would not have gotten off the ground.

For editorial and production assistance I would like to thank Carolyn Porter and Todd Meisler at New Riders who produced this manual.

To Jon C. A. DeKeles for beta testing this software and for his help in completing this project.

To Harbert Rice for his willingness to undertake the project.

And finally to Jill, Amy, Vanessa, Steve, and Melissa who put up with the long hours, and the seemingless endless "its almost finished now" progress reports.

Trademarks

Table Of Contents

A – Manager Reports

B – Installation Notes

C – Manager and Memory

I – Index

Chapter One

Introduction

Desktop Manager assists users of Xerox Ventura Publisher® to manage and controll the documents they create. Desktop Manager augments Ventura's extensive document creation and formatting features. It is fully compatible with Xerox Ventura Publisher versions 1.1 (including patches), 2.0, and 2.0 Professional Extension.

Features

Desktop Manager (Manager, for short) has been programmed in the GEM environment, providing seamless integration with Xerox Ventura Publisher. All of its features and capabilities are available from within Xerox Ventura Publisher. It provides the following features and capabilities:

Document Control: Manager lets you control the revision level of chapters and publications. You can determine when a chapter has been modified, and see the time and date of the last revision change. In addition, you can view the time and date the chapter was created, last printed, and last archived.

Chapter Information: Manager gives you access to complete chapter information. You can enter a 144-character description of each chapter, assign the chapter to a category, and enter keywords for later searches. Manager can show you the page size, orientation, and number of pages for any chapter at any time. It can display the filename, path, time, date, function, and size of each component file.

Job Tracking: This function lets you easily determine job status and schedules. In addition, you can track the writer, illustrator, editor, and manager for any chapter. This is particularly helpful in large projects where many individuals contribute to a publication.

Chapter History: Manager maintains an accurate history of significant changes and milestones for each chapter. Each time there is a revision, a chapter archive or creation, Manager logs an entry indicating the operator, time, date, and action taken. It also logs each time a chapter is printed, or each time you save a chapter.

Timed Backup: Manager can automatically save a Ventura chapter file every 5, 10, 15, or 30 minutes. This means when you are engrossed in writing or editing, Manager will save your valuable data from system or software failure.

File Management: You can copy, move, delete, and rename any file, including chapters, publications, text files, graphic files, and style sheets. In addition, you can create and remove directories using this function. Manager gives you complete control over which files are changed and which ones stay behind — even width table files. And all without leaving the Ventura work session.

Printed Reports: You can receive a printed report on any chapter or publication. A sophisticated query function lets you print a report on any chapter of a specified type, or marked with a particular keyword. PostScript, HP Laser Jet, and DOS text printers are supported. A predesigned report format is provided, or you can create your own report style. You can also create a report in disk file format, complete with tags, which you can load and format as a Ventura document.

Manager has been designed to control and manage a large number of chapters and publications. It extends the Ventura's usefulness in a natural and easy-to-use manner while bringing features and capabilities previously only found in dedicated document processing systems.

How to Use This Manual

This manual describes Manager's features, the steps to install it, and how to use it once installed. The following chapters are outlined below.

Chapter 2 - Installation: In most instances, Chapter 2 will contain all of the information necessary to successfully install Manager. Appendix B contains additional information for nonstandard Ventura installations.

Chapter 3 - Getting Started: Chapter 3 contains a short tutorial to acquaint you with Desktop Manager.

Chapter 4 - Manager Functions: A detailed description of each Manager function is contained in Chapter 4. Use this chapter as a reference tool.

Appendix A - Manager Reports: Appendix A contains a complete discussion of Manager's report capabilities. In addition, it shows you how to customize the standard reports to suit your needs.

Appendix B - Installation Notes: Appendix B contains additional information to help you install Desktop Manager in nonstandard systems. If you have installed Xerox Ventura Publisher in the \VENTURA directory, and have not modified the VP.BAT file created when Ventura was installed, Desktop Manager can be installed automatically. However, if you have modified the standard Ventura environment or batch file, a certain amount of manual installation may be necessary. Appendix B will provide you with the information you'll need to accomplish this task.

Appendix C - Manager and Memory: This Appendix presents some solutions to any memory problems you might experience with your system.

Once you've installed Desktop Manager, it will automatically load itself and then load Ventura each time you type VPMAN.BAT.

This manual only covers Desktop Manager. You can learn more about Xerox Ventura Publisher through the documentation you received with that program. However, the best sources for mastering Ventura are the books INSIDE XEROX VENTURA PUBLISHER and PUBLISHING POWER WITH VENTURA published by New Rider's Publishing. The manual assumes that you are familiar with the basic Ventura operations, such as creating and saving a chapter. If you are installing Manager and Xerox Ventura Publisher at the same time, it is recommended that you first master the basics of Ventura before tackling Manager.

Chapter Two

Installation

This chapter explains how to use Manager's automatic installation program. If you have a nonstandard installation, or you have modified the VP.BAT program, refer to Appendix B instead.

Desktop Manager is installed in the same directory as Xerox Ventura Publisher. For example, if you have installed Xerox Ventura Publisher on disk drive C:, the Manager program files will be stored in the C:\VENTURA subdirectory.

Manager runs with Ventura versions 1.1, 2.0 or 2.0 Professional Extension. If you are still using version 1.0 of the program, you must upgrade before installing Manager.

Running the Install Program

Manager's installation program takes care of all aspects of installation, including loading the program files onto your hard disk, and copying the example files into the TYPESET directory. The program comes with a set of Chapter Information Files (.CIF) for each of the standard example chapters included with Xerox Ventura Publisher. If these files are present on your system, corresponding .CIF files will be copied to the hard disk automatically.

The first step is to make a backup copy of the Master diskette. Use the DOS DISKCOPY utility. Put the Master diskette in a safe place, and use the working diskette to install the Manager program.

Insert the working diskette in Drive A:. Change the current drive to A: by entering

```
A: [Enter]
```

at the DOS prompt. Then start the installation program by typing

```
A:INSTALL [Enter]
```

The installation program will display the screen shown in Figure 2-1. You will be prompted for the letter of the disk drive containing Xerox Ventura Publisher. Enter the drive label. For example, if Xerox Ventura Publisher is installed on Drive C:, enter

```
C
```

From here on, the program requires no additional interaction. The program files will be transferred to the VENTURA directory on your disk drive followed by the example files.

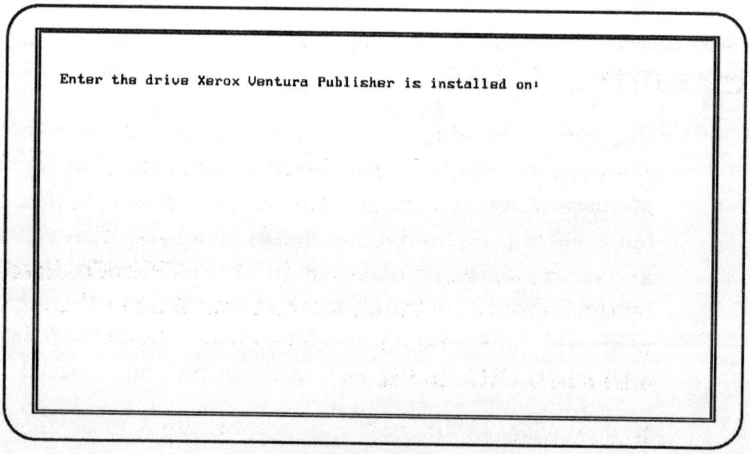

Figure 2-1

If you have any problems with installation, it may have to do with the way you configured Ventura. There is further help in Appendix B.

Loading Manager

To load Ventura *without* Manager, type VP at the DOS prompt (VPPROF if you use the Professional Extension).

To load Ventura *with* Manager, type VPMAN at the DOS prompt. The same command works regardless of the Ventura version you are using.

Once you have installed Manager, it loads automatically each time you type VPMAN. After loading itself, it loads Xerox Ventura Publisher for you. The program is co-resident with Ventura, and is automatically removed from memory each time you exit Xerox Ventura Publisher.

☞ *WARNING: Manager captures the operator's initials and records them in the chapter history. If you ran Ventura without Manager, you will defeat part of its purpose. Once you have installed Manager, we recommend that you always start Ventura by typing VPMAN.*

Example Files

Chapter 3 contains a tutorial based around the example chapters distributed with Xerox Ventura Publisher. Your Manager distribution diskette contains a sample .CIF file for each of the standard example chapters. These standard examples were installed in the TYPESET directory by the Ventura installation program. Most of them begin with the ampersand character — &BOOK-P1.CAP, &LTR1-P1.CHP and so on.

If you wish to have Manager's example .CIF files installed, but have erased their associated chapter files, you must re-install the chapter files before installing Manager.

To re-install the Xerox Ventura Publisher example chapters, you must re-install Xerox Ventura Publisher itself.

Report Style Sheet

Desktop Manager can print a report to a pretagged file. The report can be read into Xerox Ventura Publisher, edited if desired, and printed. A companion style sheet is included. This file, REPORT.STY, is automatically installed in the \TYPESET directory on the drive that contains Ventura.

Invoking Manager with Hot Keys

The Desktop Manager functions are invoked using three *hot keys*:

Alt-D for document functions
Alt-F for file management functions
Alt-T for the timed backup feature

Just like Ventura, Manager gets its keyboard input from GEM, rather than directly from the keyboard. Therefore, if you are using a Terminate-and-Stay-Resident (TSR) program, and it works with Ventura, it will probably work with Manager, providing of course, that there is sufficient RAM in your system for everybody.

Because Ventura Version 2.0 is a large program, there is a good chance it may not load with Manager and another TSR program. In that case, remove the TSR before typing VPMAN.

Because Ventura's Professional Extension can use expanded memory (EMS), it may be easier to run other TSR programs together with Manager and Ventura.

If your TSR uses any of the Manager key sequences (Alt-D, Alt-F, or Alt-T), you may need to reconfigure your TSR, or remove it from memory when running Xerox Ventura Publisher and Manager.

Chapter Three

Getting Started

This chapter contains a tutorial on the use of Desktop Manager. It is based around example .CIF files provided with Manager. These files are automatically installed in the \TYPESET directory if Ventura's example chapters are present.

This tutorial should not take you more than 10 to 15 minutes to complete. It acquaints you with Manager's major features. This chapter is not intended as a reference section. Instead, it tries to quickly familiarize you with the basic operating characteristics. Chapter 4 contains a complete description of each Desktop Manager function.

Booting Manager

After Manager has been installed, the dialog box shown in Figure 3-1 will be displayed each time you type VPMAN at the DOS prompt. Remember, You don't have to load Ventura separately. Once you type VPMAN, Manager loads both itself and Ventura. You will be prompted for a User ID. Type your initials — or any combination of up to three letters and/or numbers — onto the line. Press Return and Ventura will load as usual.

Figure 3-1

The User ID shows who does what. Manager keeps track of chapter creation, printing, saving, and revision levels. Each of these activities has a User ID associated with it.

Manager Modes

The three hot keys Alt-D, Alt-F, and Alt-T will invoke the Manager modes: Document Management, File Management, and Timed Backup.

You will use Document Management to track, organize, and oversee your work. It includes:

- chapter information
- document control
- job tracking
- chapter and publication selection
- style sheet information

In file management mode you can copy, move, delete, and rename files, chapters, publications, or style sheets. In addition, you can create and delete directories.

Time Backup mode is an important safety feature. You use this mode to enable or disable this function, or to choose the timed interval (Figure 3-2).

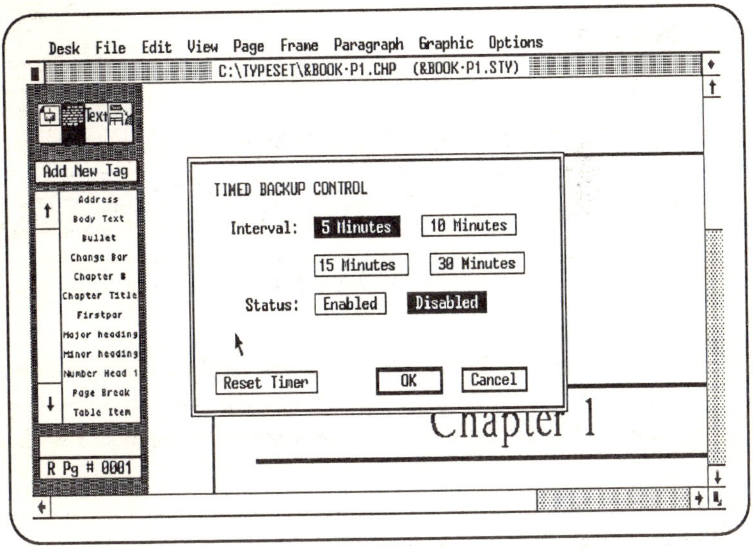

Figure 3-2

Tutorial

Let's start with a quick tour. Load Manager and Ventura by typing VPMAN. Enter your ID (your initials) when prompted. When Ventura is loaded, open the &BOOK-P1.CHP in the TYPESET directory. This is one of the example files distributed with the Xerox Ventura Publisher package.

☞ *NOTE: If you did not install Ventura's example chapters, or if you have moved or deleted them, you must re-install them, then re-install Manager to run this tutorial.*

Let's look at some data for this chapter. Enter an Alt-D to select the document management mode.

Your screen should look like Figure 3-3. Notice that all five of the function buttons are enabled. Each time you open a chapter under Xerox Ventura Publisher, Manager will automatically make it the *active* chapter. If we had begun this exercise without opening a chapter in Ventura, there would be no active chapter, and only the Select function would be enabled.

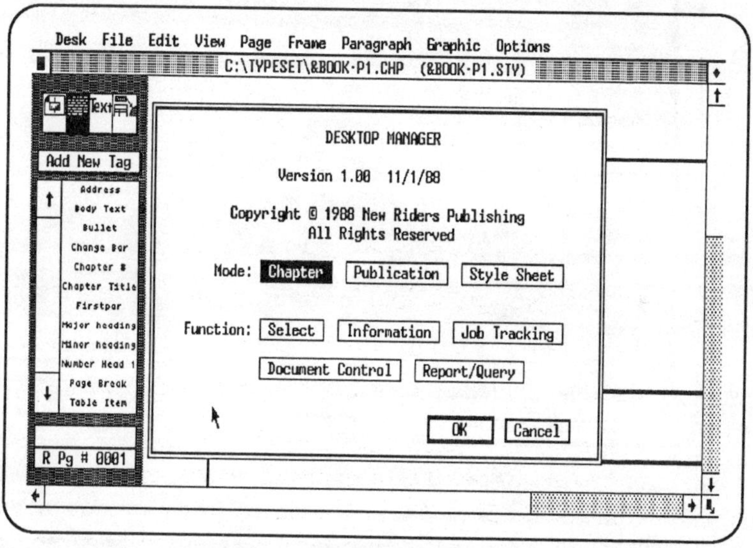

Figure 3-3

Lets try each function in turn.

Document Control

Select the Document Control function by clicking on the Document Control button. The Document Control dialog box is displayed. (Figure 3-4)

Notice that there is no name after the label Publication:, and all the buttons related to a publication are disabled (displayed in gray).

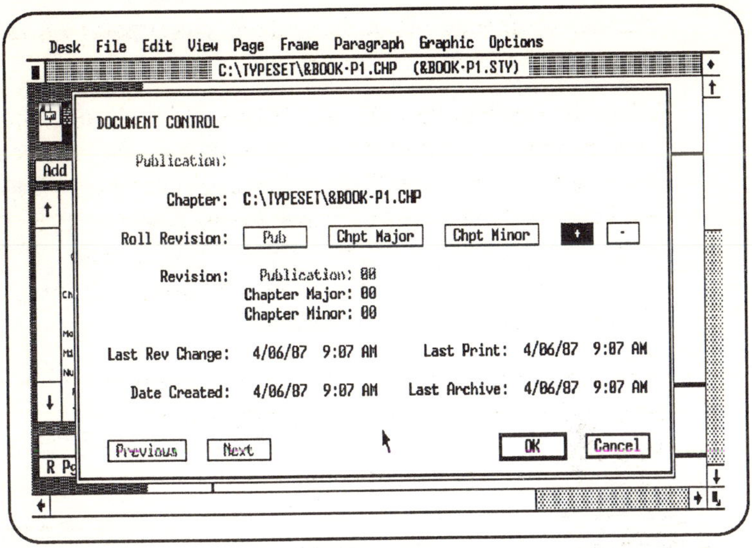

Figure 3-4

- the Pub button on the Roll Revision line
- the Publication line in the Revision Section
- the Previous and Next buttons at the bottom left

These buttons are only active in Publication mode.

The screen indicates that the &BOOK-P1.CHP chapter is at revision level 00. In addition, you'll see that Last Rev Change and Date Created read 4/06/87 9:07 AM. Revision level 00. means the rev level has never been changed. Therefore, the chapter's creation date shows the Last Rev Change field.

Let's change the current revision level to 01. Click on the Chpt Major button.

The Chapter Major revision level now displays as 01. The chapter revision level is made up of two components, the Major and Minor revision level. (These are joined together into a single revision level elsewhere in the program.) The chapter is now at revision level 1.00 (Chapter Major level 1 and Chapter Minor level 00). The numbers in front of the decimal point represent major revisions. The numbers after the decimal point represent minor revisions.

Each dialog box has a Cancel and an OK button. Changes do not take effect until you click OK. To undo changes, select Cancel instead.

Record the new revision level by clicking OK. Manager now returns you to the main dialog box.

Enter the Document Control function again to confirm that your changes were incorporated. Click on Document Control. The dialog box reappears (Figure 3-5).

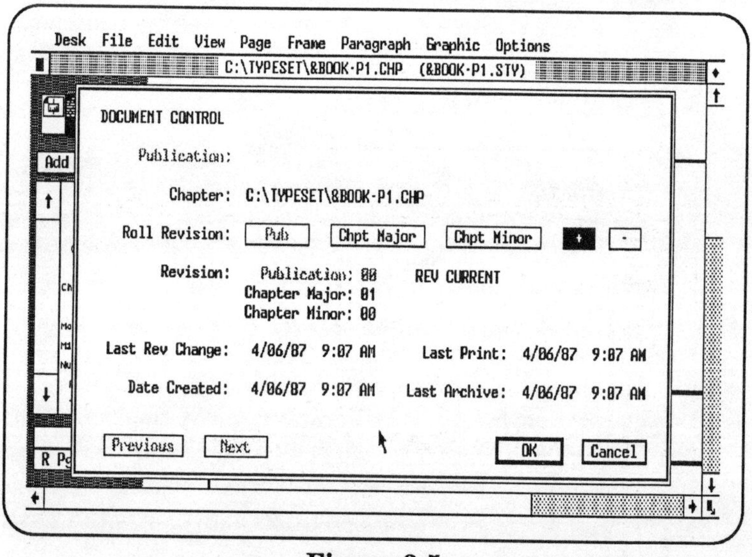

Figure 3-5

You'll notice in Figure 3-5 that the revision level now shows as 01 and the words Rev Current now appears. The Rev Current indicator is displayed whenever the chapter file's time and date match the time and date of the last revision change. This indicates whether the chapter file has been altered since the last time the revision level was changed. If you were to exit Manager and save the chapter, then re-enter the Document Control function, the Rev Current indicator will not display because the chapter had been changed since the last time the revision was rolled.

Note that the time and date of the Last Rev Change are still shown as 4/06/87 and 9:07 AM. This is correct. Each time the revision level is altered, the *time and date of the chapter file are used, rather than the current system time and date*.

Now click OK to return to Manager's main dialog box.

Chapter Information

Let's look at the Chapter Information function.

Click on the Information button while Chapter is highlighted in the main dialog box. The Chapter Information dialog box shown in Figure 3-6 appears.

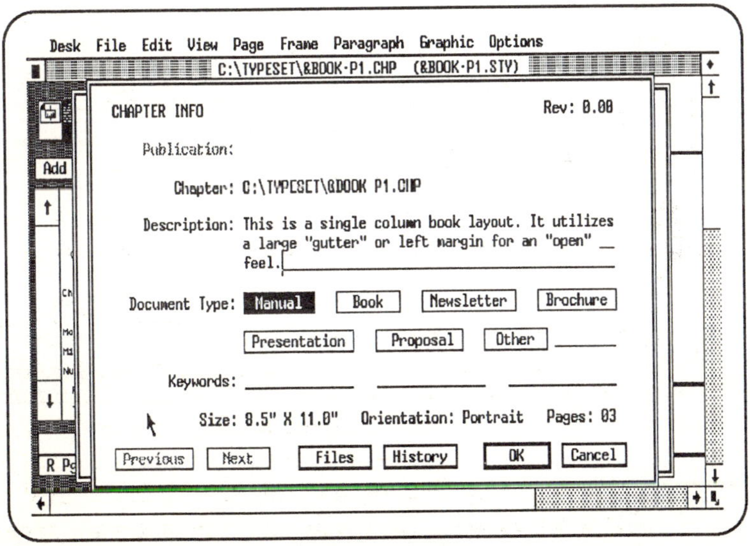

Figure 3-6

The cursor is located at the end of the first line of the description. Use the backspace key to erase the entire line, then re-enter the information. Now move to the next line of the description using the Tab key. You can erase any text field in Manager or Xerox Ventura Publisher using the Esc key. Press the Esc key to erase the second line of the description and retype the text. You can move back a field by holding down either of the Shift keys, then pressing the Tab key. Move to the first line of the description again. Experiment some more with entering text.

File Data

Chapter Information has two important subfunctions. Let's examine the File Data subfunction first, then proceed to Chapter History.

Click on the Files button to invoke the File Data subfunction (Figure 3-7).

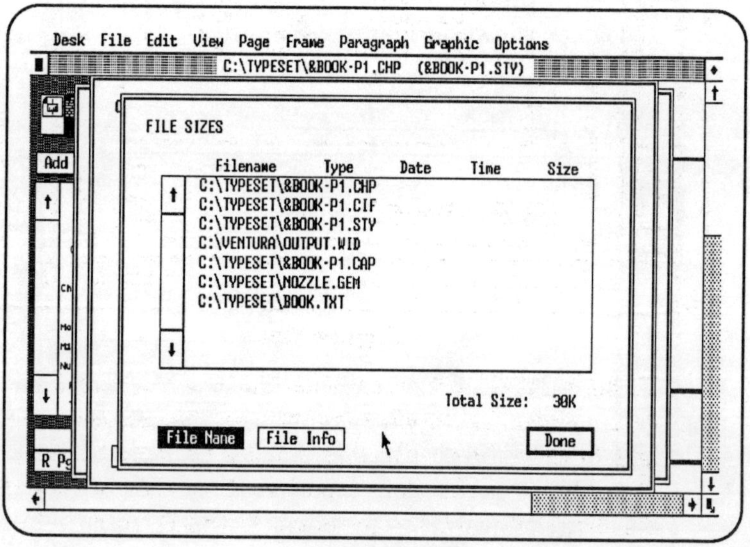

Figure 3-7

You can view data in two different formats. The default format displays the path and filename of each file in the chapter (Figure 3-7).

Unlike the Multi-Chapter function in Xerox Ventura Publisher, Manager displays all of the component files, including graphics (.VGR), caption (.CAP), chapter (.CHP), chapter information (.CIF), style sheet (.STY), width table (.WID), as well as text, images, and line-art files.

Click on the File Info button at the bottom of the dialog box to see the second file display format. Now the component files show the file type, time and date, and file size (Figure 3-8).

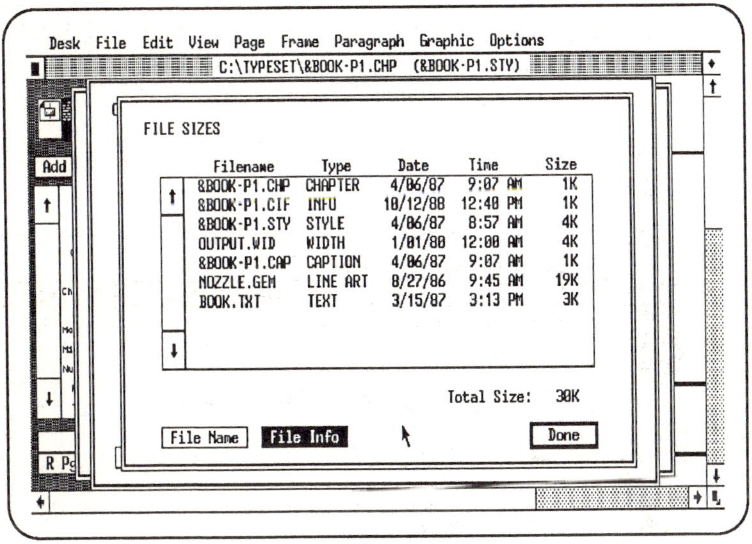

Figure 3-8

If the number of files exceeds ten, use the scroll arrows or the slider bar to view the others. You can switch back and forth between the two display formats to view the data. When you're done experimenting with the file data display, click on Done to return to the Chapter Information dialog box.

Chapter History

The second subfunction supported by Chapter Information is Chapter History. It is often useful to determine the history of a chapter file — when it was created, printed, saved, and revised. In addition, if more than one individual is working on the chapter, it is helpful to track who did what, when.

Each time you load Manager, you are asked to enter your ID. This ID becomes part of the chapter history. Whenever a chapter is created, the revision rolled, printed, or saved, an entry is automatically made in the Chapter History record. You can review a chapter's history by clicking on History at the bottom of the Chapter Information dialog box.

The Chapter History dialog box shown in Figure 3-9 appears. You should see a CREATED entry, as well as the Roll Revision entries from the earlier portion of this tutorial. These revisions will display your initials.

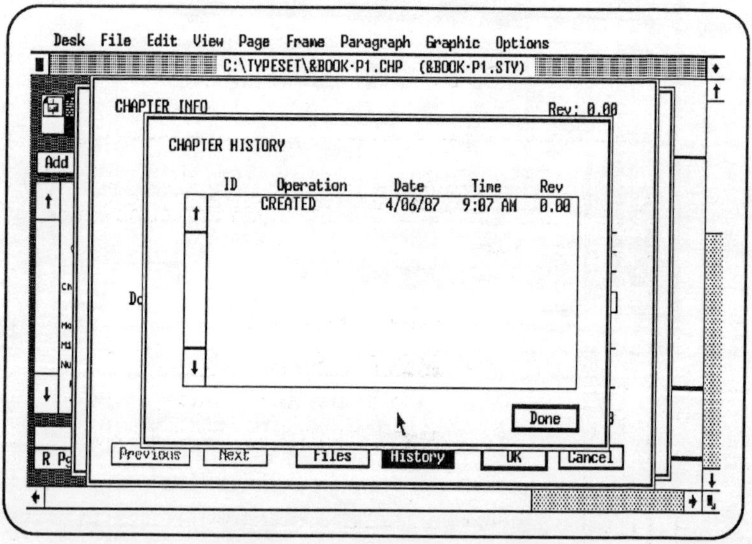

Figure 3-9

You will notice there is no ID before the CREATED record. Chapter files created without Manager do not have an Operator ID. This situation arises with chapters already in existence on your system when you install Manager, or with chapters created when Manager has been disabled (see Appendix B).

As with the File Data, only ten entries can be displayed at a time. If more entries are present, you can view them using the up arrow, down arrow, or slider bar.

When you are done reviewing Chapter History data, click on Done to return to the Chapter Information dialog box.

We've reviewed all of the Chapter Information, File Data, and Chapter History features. Click on OK to return to Manager's main dialog box.

Job Tracking

In large publications or jobs where more than one individual is involved, it is helpful to track the progress and status of a project. The Job Tracking function gives you this ability.

Click on the Job Tracking button in the main dialog box to display the Job Tracking dialog box. Figure 3-10 shows the data for the &BOOK-P1 chapter.

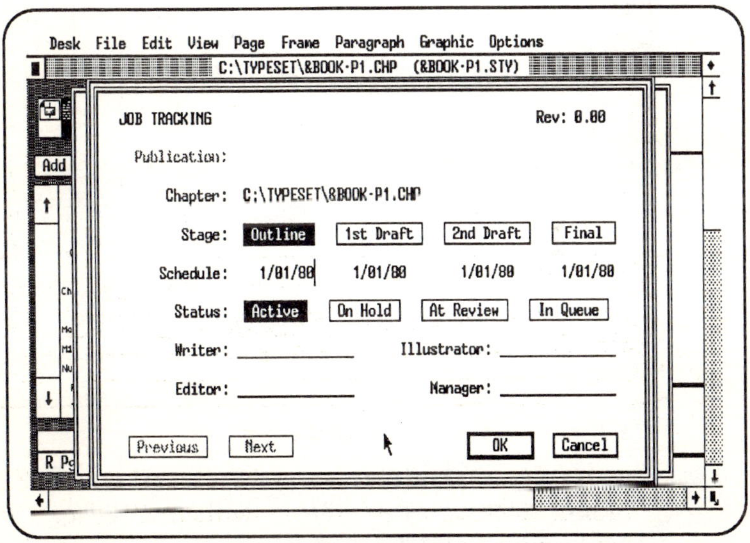

Figure 3-10

The first set of buttons (Stage:) indicates the chapter's stage of completion. Select the button that most accurately describes the current status of the job. Each button has a date field beneath it to facilitate project planning. You can enter a date to correspond to the expected comly describes the current status of the job. Each button has a date field beneath it to facilitate project planning. You can enter a date to correspond to the expected completion date for that stage. This date shows in the printed reports to help managers track progress.

Below the schedule fields are four buttons to help keep track of the current status of each chapter file. When large publications are produced, individual chapters change status frequently.

The final four fields are for the names of the individuals involved in the projects. Enter the names as you entered the chapter descriptions. You can move between the schedule date and name fields using the Tab and Shift-Tab keys You can edit any existing data using the Backspace and Esc keys.

Change the stage, status indicators, schedule, and name fields until you are comfortable entering data. Then click OK to return to the Manager's main dialog box.

Report/Query Function

The Report/Query function prints a report with all the information on a chapter or a publication. Select it by clicking on the Report button in the main dialog box. The dialog box shown in Figure 3-11 displays.

Select the printer type and output port that corresponds to your printer. If you wish to print the report to disk, instead of directly to the printer, select the Filename button. If you choose Ventura, the report will go to a file which you can load and format using the supplied style sheet or a style sheet of your own.

For our tutorial, a report containing all of the chapter information for the &BOOK-P1 chapter will be printed as soon as you click OK. After the report is printed, Manager returns you to the main dialog box.

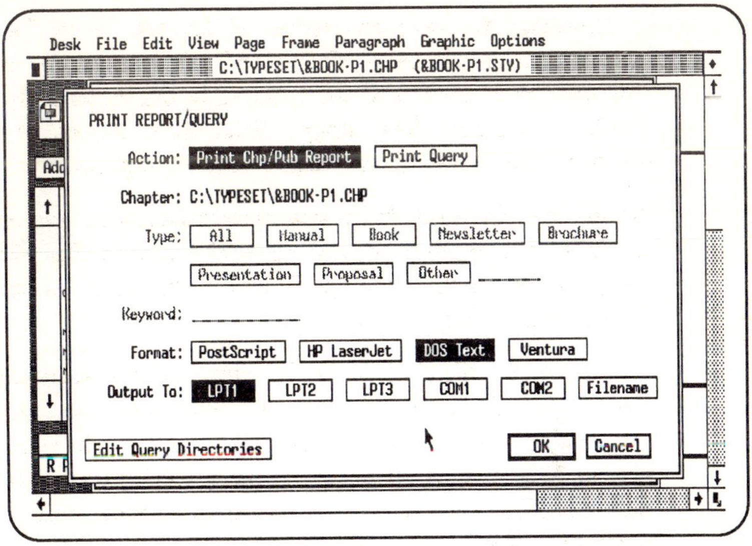

Figure3-11

Selecting a New Chapter

Now that we've reviewed the capabilities of Manager using the &BOOK-P1 chapter, let's learn to select a different chapter. The Select function chooses the chapter or publication file you want Manager to work with. We are currently in the chapter mode (indicated by the Chapter button displayed in reverse video in the main dialog box), so this function will select another chapter for us.

Click on the Select button. You now see the familiar Ventura Item Selector. You select chapters in Manager the same way you do in Ventura.

Select the SCOOP chapter by double-clicking on SCOOP.CHP. Manager returns you to the main dialog box, with SCOOP.CHP selected as the active chapter. Now you can select any of the functions or subfunctions you've just explored to review the chapter information for the SCOOP chapter. Try it on your own. When you've finished exploring, return to the main dialog box.

Publication Mode

Publication mode is similar to Chapter mode, except that you have access to all the chapters within a publication.

Select Publication mode by clicking on the Publication button in the main dialog box. Then, select a publication file. All of Manager functions except Select are disabled when you enter Publication mode until you select the publication you want to work with.

Click on the Select button. Ventura's Item Selector now displays publication files rather than chapter files. You should see at least one publication file in the TYPESET directory: &EXAMPLE.PUB. Select this publication.

Manager returns you to the main dialog box. Now the function buttons are available because you have an active publication.

All of Manager's functions and subfunctions work the same in Publication mode as in Chapter mode. However, the two buttons, Previous and Next (in the lower left) are now active. These buttons let you move from one chapter to another within the publication.

Select the Document Control subfunction. You'll notice that the dialog box has changed slightly since the last time you saw it. The name of the publication (&EXAMPLE.PUB) is displayed at the top of the dialog box as shown in Figure 3-12. Below that the chapter file is identified as CAPABILI.CHP. Each time a publication is opened, the first chapter file in that publication becomes the active chapter. Since CAPABILI.CHP is the first chapter file in the publication &EXAMPLE.PUB, it becomes the active chapter.

The Previous button is disabled and the Next button is enabled. The buttons refer to the chapter files contained within the publication. You are at the first chapter in the publication file, so there is no previous chapter. Hence, the Previous button is not active.

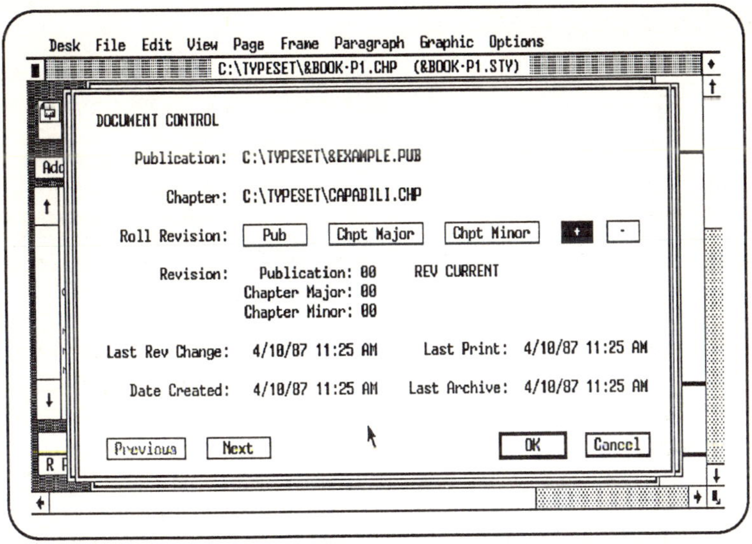

Figure 3-12

Click on the Next button to review the Document Control data for the second chapter file in the publication.

Now Previous is enabled because there is now a chapter before the existing one. If you continue clicking the Next button, you will advance one chapter at a time to the end of the publication. When the last chapter has been selected, the Next button is disabled, because there are no more chapters in the publication file.

As you move from chapter to chapter you can enter or edit the active chapter's information. You can enter or edit data exactly the same way you did in the Chapter mode, with one important difference.

☞ *While in the Document Control function, you must click the OK button in order to update the chapter information file.*

☞ *For example, if you are in Document Control, and you change the chapter's revision level, you must click OK to record this change in the chapter's information file.*

If you omit this step and click on Next instead, Manager ignores the new data.

Once you are done experimenting with the Manager functions in Publication mode, return to the main dialog box. Now click OK and you will be returned to Xerox Ventura Publisher.

File Management

You can access File Management during a Ventura work session with the Alt-F key sequence.

Type Alt-F. The File Management dialog box shown in Figure 3-13 displays.

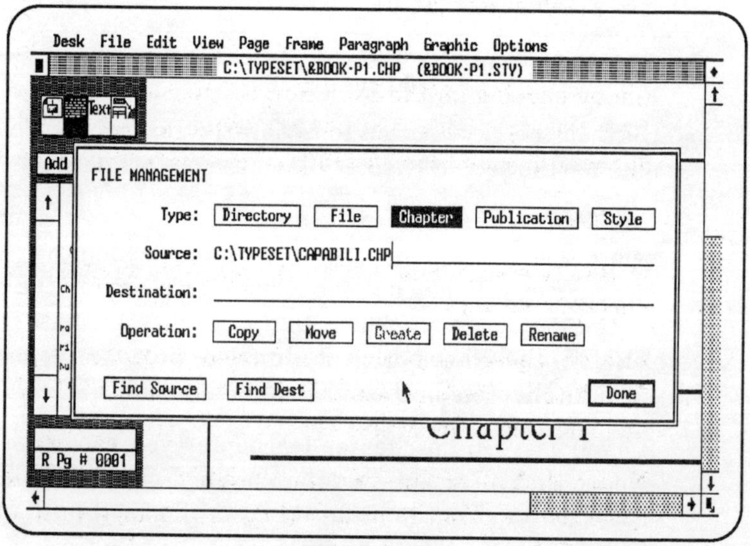

Figure 3-13

File Management consist of five operations:

- copy
- move
- create
- delete
- rename

Let's start by creating a directory that you'll use later for copying files and chapters. The first step is to select the type of operation.

Click the Directory button.

You'll notice that all of the operation buttons except Create and Delete are disabled (displayed in gray), since it is not possible to copy, move, or rename a directory.

Next, select the name of the directory you wish to create. For this tutorial, you will create a subdirectory call TEST in the \TYPESET directory. You can enter the specification directly on the Source line as

```
C:\TYPESET\TEST
```

or you can use the Ventura Item Selector to specify the file by clicking on the Find Source button. If you use the Item Selector, click Find Source. When the Item Selector appears, move to the \TYPESET directory and enter

```
TEST
```

in the Selection field. Click OK. Manager creates the requested directory.

Now that you have created a directory, try moving some files into it. Click on the File button to indicate that you are selecting a file operation.

Notice that all of the Operation buttons except Create become active. This indicates that you can perform copy, move, delete, and rename operations on a file.

As when creating a directory, you must enter the name of the file(s) you want to copy, move, delete, or rename. You can either type them directly into the Source line, or you can use the Item Selector. For instance, to select all files in the TYPESET directory with the filename of &BOOK-P1 by typing

```
C:\TYPESET\&BOOK-P1.*
```

directly into the Source field, or use the Item Selector to move into the C:\TYPESET directory to enter &BOOK-P1.* into the Selection field.

Once you have selected the files to copy, select the destination. If you wish to rename the files, you must enter the new name on the Destination line. For this tutorial, enter the TEST directory you created earlier. (C:\TYPESET\TEST\).

☞ *NOTE: You must specify a destination to copy, move, or rename. The only operation that doesn't require a destination is delete.*

Once you've selected the source, destination, and type of operation, as shown in Figure 3-14, click OK. Manager copies the files &BOOK-P1.CHP, &BOOK-P1.CAP, &BOOK-P1.STY, and &BOOK-P1.CIF to the C:\TYPESET\TEST\.

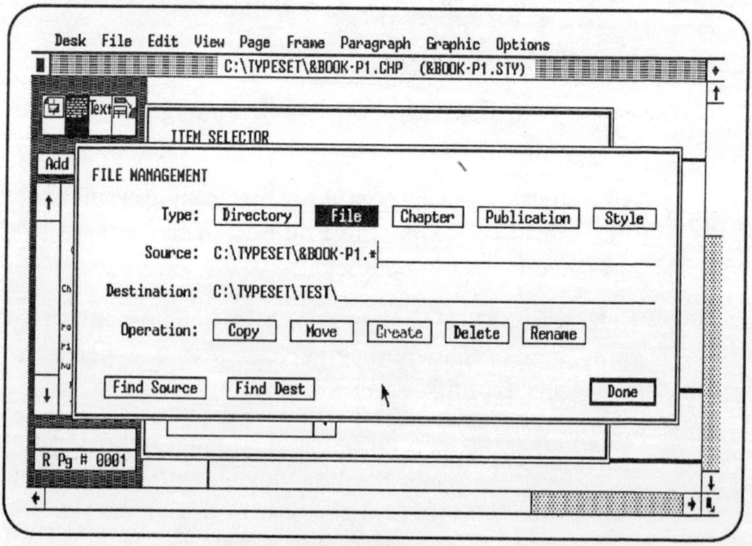

Figure 3-14

Now try moving a chapter. Lets copy &BOOK-P1.CHP into the C:\TYPESET\TEST directory.

Click on the Chapter button. Select the chapter with the Item Selector or by typing the name on the Source line. Next, select C:\TYPESET\TEST\ as the destination. Select the copy operation by clicking on the Copy button. Click OK.

Manager displays the screen shown in Figure 3-15. This dialog box lets you indicate whether or not the component files should be copied.

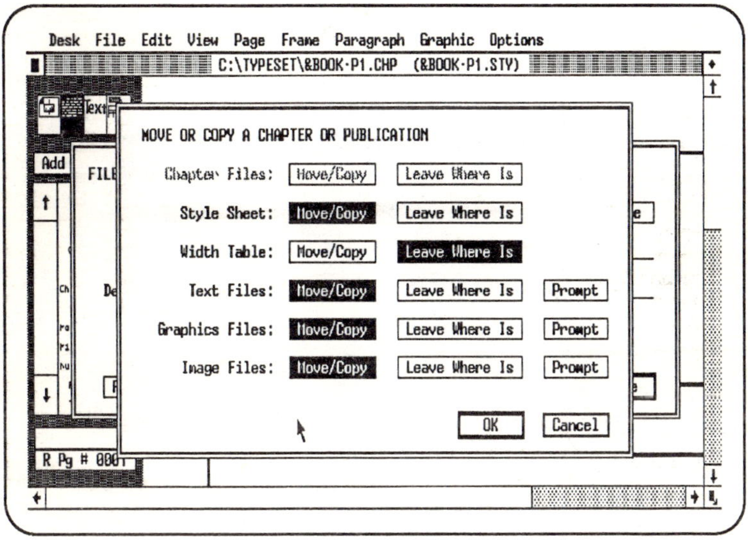

Figure 3-15

☞ *NOTE: You will usually want to leave the width table in the \VENTURA directory, to avoid littering the disk with extra copies of this file.*

Three classes of component files (text, graphics, and image files), can be copied or left alone. Also, you can ask Manager to prompt you for each file in the category, allowing you to move some, but not all, component files for any given chapter.

Once you've specified which files you want copied, and clicked OK, the dialog box shown in Figure 3-16 appears.

In this dialog box you can specify which directory you want the files to be copied into. Initially all of the lines show the directory you specified earlier as the destination (C:\TYPESET\TEST\), but you can change some or all of these if you wish.

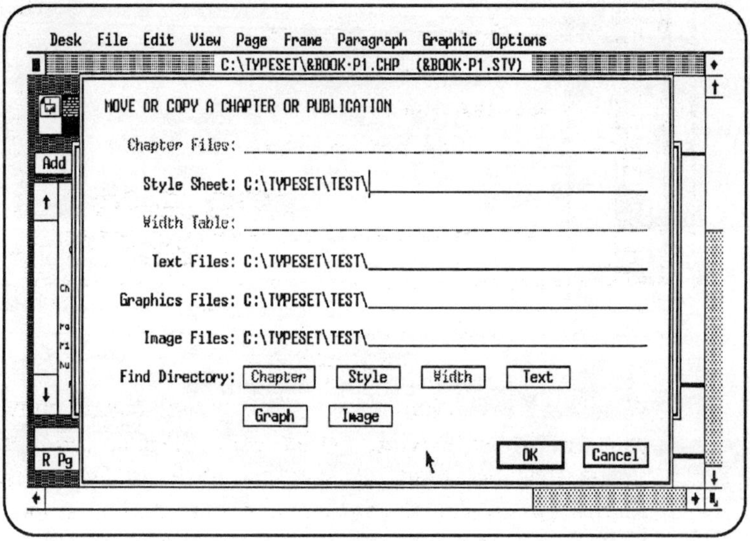

Figure 3-16

You can type in a directory path directly, or you can click on the corresponding button at the bottom of the screen, and use the Item Selector. For example, to change the destination directory for text files, click on Text. An Item Selector appears with which you can select the new destination. Once you've altered any of the destination directories, click OK to begin the copy operation.

Since you've already copied the &BOOK-P1 files into this directory while exploring the file copy operation, Manager detects a file conflict. The dialog box shown in Figure 3-17 displays.

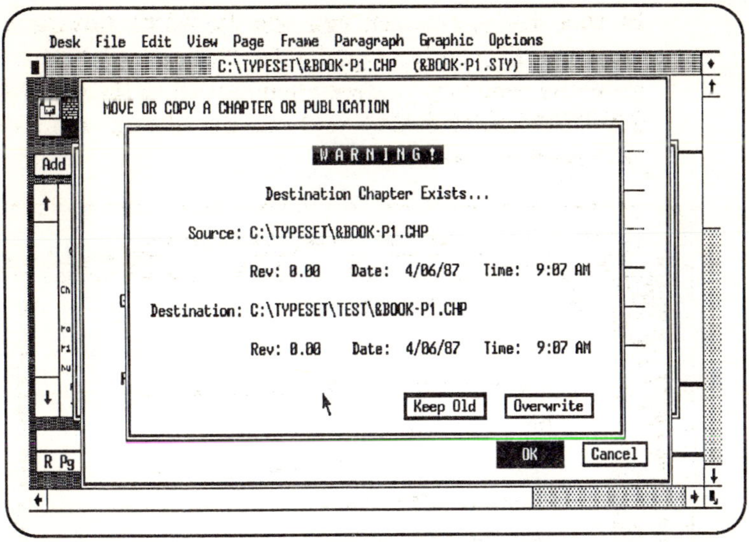

Figure 3-17

Whenever a conflict occurs, this dialog box displays so you can indicate what action you'd like to take. Since these files are identical, you can click on Overwrite or Keep Old, whichever you'd like. This same dialog box will display for each of the four files which were already in the directory. When Manager is done copying, it returns to the File Management main dialog box (Figure 3-13).

The two other file types, publications and style sheets, operate identically to the chapters and files, respectively.

This concludes the Manager tutorial. Chapter 4 contains a complete description of all Manager functions. If you have specific questions about any Manager operation, consult that chapter.

NOTES

Chapter Four

Desktop Manager Functions

This chapter contains a complete explanation of all Desktop Manager commands and functions. It assumes that you are familiar with Xerox Ventura Publisher, and its user interface. For example, Manager uses the same Item Selector used by Ventura. If you are unfamiliar with these topics, we suggest you review the Xerox Ventura Publisher Training Guide or Reference Manual.

Selecting a Manager Mode

Manager has three separate modes that can be selected using the Alt-D, Alt-T, and Alt-F key sequences. The first is Document Management. This mode lets you control document revision levels, obtain extensive information about a chapter, and track the progress of a project. We will discuss this mode first.

The second mode, Timed Backup, automatically backs up your document on a periodic basis. In this chapter, we'll show you how to enable and disable Timed Backup, as well as alter the interval between backups.

Manager's third mode, File Management, provides extensive file management tools. You can copy, move, delete, and rename files, chapters, style sheets, and publications. In addition you can create and delete directories. File Management is described at the end of this chapter.

Document Management

Document Management (Alt-D) has three distinct modes of operation — Chapter, Publication, and Style Sheet. Chapter operations work with chapter information. This is the default mode for Document Management. In publication mode, you access the same functions, but for an entire publication, not just a single chapter. The Style Sheet mode provides data about the tags in a specific Ventura style sheet.

You select the operation with the Mode buttons at the top of the dialog box (Figure 4-1). To change the selected mode, simply click on a different button.

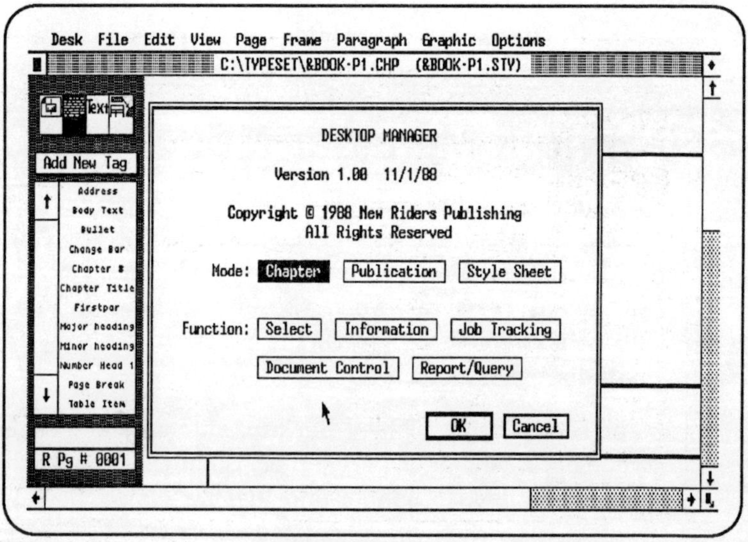

Figure 4-1

Below the mode buttons, there are five function buttons. Some of these buttons may be disabled, depending on the mode selected.

Select File

You must select an active file before you can use any of the Document Management functions. You can determine whether you have an active file by examining the state of the buttons. If they are disabled (displayed in gray), Manager does not yet have an active file.

Selecting a File

If you open Document Management while working on a Ventura chapter, Manager assumes that this is the chapter you want to work on.

To select another file, click on the Select button. The Item Selector appears (Figure 4-2).

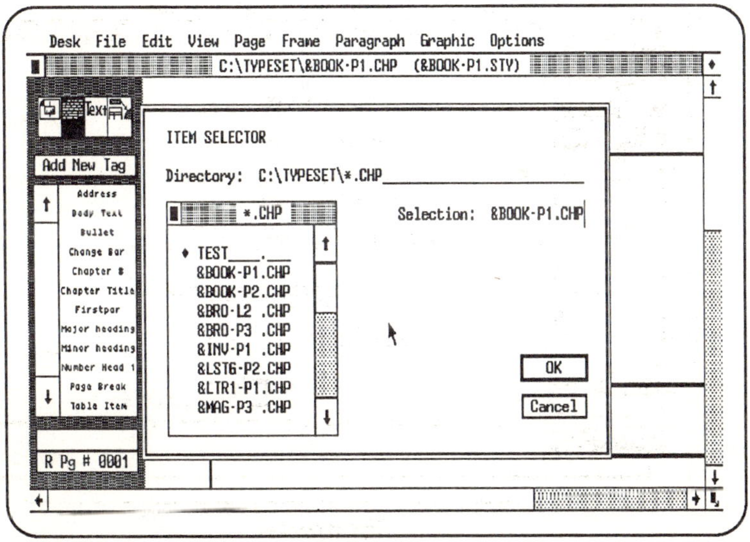

Figure 4-2

The Item Selector operates the same in Manager as in Xerox Ventura Publisher. If you are unfamiliar with its operation, please consult the Xerox Ventura Publisher Reference manual.

The Item Selector is automatically set to look for .CHP files in Chapter mode, .PUB files in Publication mode, and .STY files in the Style Sheet mode. The Item Selector starts in the last directory you accessed for a file type, whether with Xerox Ventura Publisher or with Manager.

For example, if you open a chapter in the C:\TYPESET directory with Xerox Ventura Publisher, the Item Selector will start in the same directory under Manager. Likewise, if you select a chapter in C:\MANUAL under Manager, then wish to make another chapter active, the C:\MANUAL directory will be your starting point.

If you use the Select function before opening a chapter Manager starts at the directory saved by Xerox Ventura Publisher from the previous work session (stored in the Xerox Ventura Publisher info file).

Active Files

Manager has been designed to follow as closely as possible your activity within Xerox Ventura Publisher. However, under certain situations Manager will automatically select an active file in Chapter and Style Sheet modes.

When you open a chapter in Ventura, Manager makes this chapter active, superceding any others.

Likewise, Manager automatically selects a chapter when you switch from Publication mode back to Chapter mode. When you make a Publication active with Publication mode, Manager also makes the first chapter of that publication active. If you switch back to Chapter mode, the active chapter stays active. You can, of course, choose a different chapter.

In Publication mode, you must always select a publication before using any of Manager's functions.

Style Sheet mode always has an active file. It will be either the active Ventura style sheet, or the style sheet for the active chapter in the Chapter or Publication modes. You can change it if you wish to work in a different mode.

Document Control

The Document Control function lets you set and control the revision level of your documents. Once you have selected a Chapter or Publication, you can invoke Document Control by clicking the Document Control button in the main dialog box. The Document Control dialog box appears (Figure 4-3).

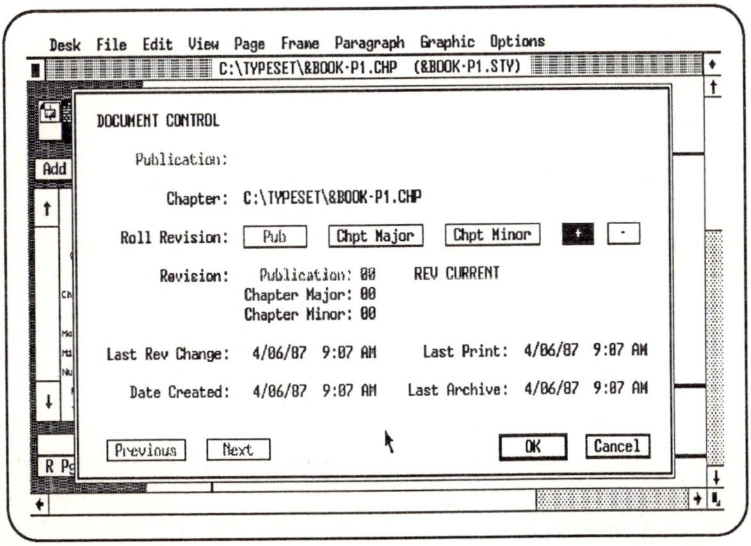

Figure 4-3

Document Control Fields

The Document Control dialog box contains the fields described below.

Publication: This field contains the file specification for the active publication in the Publication mode. If you are in the Chapter mode, the label is disabled, and the field is blank.

Chapter: This field displays the current chapter. If you are in the Chapter mode, it contains the file specification of the active chapter. In Publication mode, it shows the file specification of the current component chapter. (Publication mode allows you to cycle between all the chapters in the publication.)

Roll Revision: The Roll Revision buttons alter the revision levels of the chapter or publication. In Publication mode, all three buttons are active. In Chapter mode, the Pub button is disabled. The Plus and Minus buttons control the direction of the revision change. You can increase or decrease the revision level by one (for example, 01 to 02) by clicking on a button. You can increase or decrease the revision level by ten (for example, 01 to 11) by holding down either Shift key while clicking a button.

Revision: This field displays the current revision level of the publication and chapter. In Chapter mode, the Publication revision is disabled. The Major and Minor chapter revision levels are joined together into a chapter revision level. For example, if the major revision level is 02, and the minor level is 03, the chapter revision level is 2.03. This revision level displays in several other Manager dialog boxes and reports. Note that revision levels will *roll over* not unlike an automobile odometer from 99 to 00.

Last Rev Change: This field displays the time and date the chapter revision level last changed.

Date Created: This field displays the time and date the chapter file was created.

Last Print: This field displays the time and date the chapter was last printed.

Last Archive: This field contains the time and date the chapter file was last archived.

Rolling the Chapter Revision Level

The Chapter revision can be rolled in either the Chapter or Publication mode. Using the Chpt Major, Chpt Minor, Plus, and Minus buttons, set the chapter revision to the desired level. Then click OK. Manager sets the revision level to the new level and returns to the main dialog box.

It is particularly important to click OK in Publication mode. If you alter the chapter revision, then move to another chapter in the publication without clicking on OK, the revision level remains unchanged.

Each time the chapter revision level is altered (by clicking OK), the Last Rev Change field will be updated. Keep in mind when reviewing the contents of this field that it contains the *time and date of the chapter file, not the time and date you clicked OK.*

Each time Manager displays the Document Control dialog box, it compares the time and date of the chapter file is compared with the time and date the Last Rev was changed. If they match, it means the chapter has not been modified since it was set to the current revision level. In that case, Manager displays the Rev Current indicator shown in Figure 4-4. If this indicator does not show, it means the chapter has been saved since the last time the revision level was rolled, and the chapter might be *off rev*.

As an example of the usefulness of this feature, let's review a typical scenario. You are ready to send off a chapter to the printers for offset reproduction, so you set the revision level to 1.00. After the document has been printed, you or someone else modifies the chapter. When you review the revision level in Manager, the Rev Current indicator is not displayed. the lack of the Rev Current line indicates that the chapter may not be identical to the version that was printed.

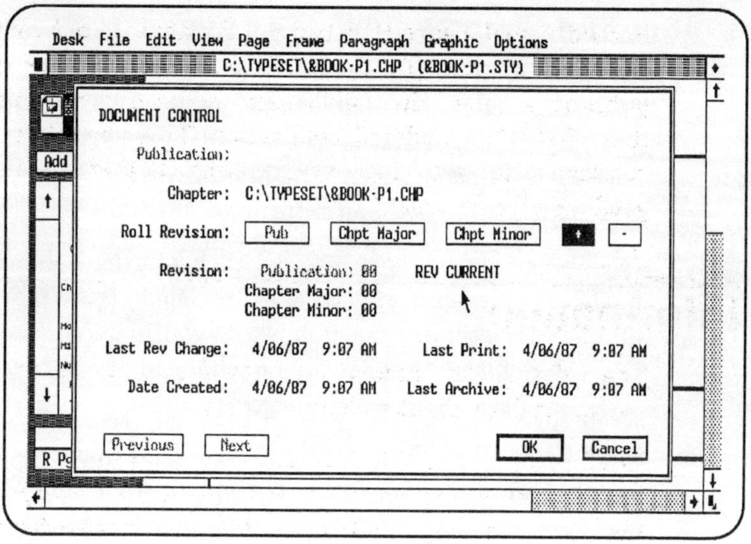

Figure 4-4

Rolling the Publication Revision Level

Manager supports revision level tracking for publications as well as chapters. In order to change the revision level of a publication you must be in the Publication mode. Set the publication revision to the desired level using the Pub, Plus, and Minus buttons, then click OK. Manager updates the publication revision level in the .CIF file of each chapter in the publication.

The publication revision level is stored in each chapter's information file because there is no support in Xerox Ventura Publisher for a publication information file. The significance is twofold. First, when you add a chapter to a publication, its publication revision level will probably not match the other chapters in the publication. Therefore, take care when adding chapters to publications.

One solution is to reset the publication revision level. For example, if the current publication revision level is 01, increase it to 02, then decrease it to 01. The publication revision level for each chapter, including the new one(s) will be set to 01.

Secondly, make sure that two publications do not contain the same chapter. If a chapter is included in two or more publication files, the publication revision level will be that of the last updated publication. This shouldn't be a common situation since overlapping chapters is not a good idea for document control.

Information

The Information function provides the ability to find out pertinent data about a chapter or style sheet.

In Chapter mode, this function displays a user-supplied description of the chapter's information on component files, and the chapter's history. The Information function works the same way in the Publication mode, except that you can cycle through all the chapters in the publication one by one.

In Style Sheet mode, the Information function displays the style sheet name and a summary of the parameters for all the tags.

We'll discuss the Information function for chapters and publications first. Then we will describe the operation of the Style Sheet Information function.

Chapter Information Fields

If you are in the Chapter or Publication mode with an active file, you can invoke the Chapter Information function by clicking on the Information button in the main dialog box. The Chapter Information dialog box appears (Figure 4-5).

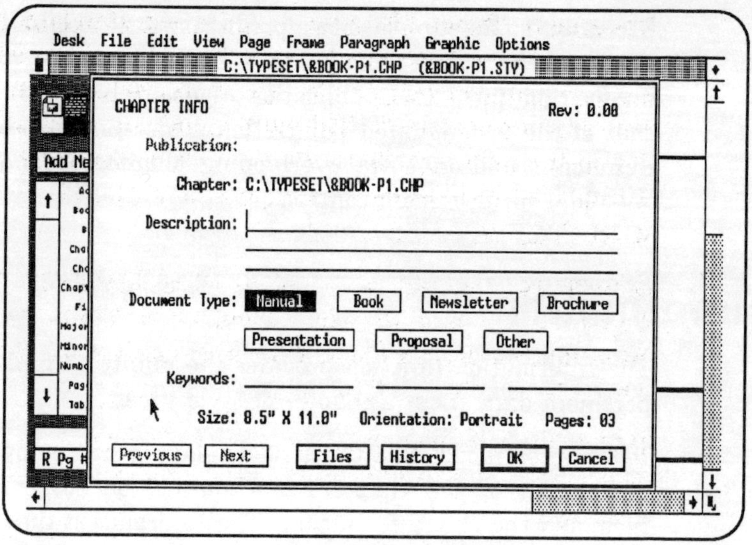

Figure 4-5

The Chapter Information dialog box contains fields described below.

Publication: This field contains the file specification for the active publication in Publication mode. In the Chapter mode, the label is disabled and the field is blank.

Chapter: This field displays the name of the current chapter. In the Chapter mode, it contains the file specification of the active chapter In Publication mode, it displays the file specification of the currently selected component chapter.

Description: The chapter description is a user-supplied description of the chapter contents. The description consists of three separate fields, one for each line. To move between the fields, press the Tab key, or use the mouse to move the text cursor to the desired location.

☞ *NOTE: Do Not use the Return key to move between lines. The Return key will exit the Chapter Information dialog box, and return you to Manager's main dialog box.*

Document Type: Manager provides six standard and one user-defined document types. You can select one of the user-defined by clicking on the appropriate button. Or you can click on the OTHER button, and enter a description in the field directly to the right. The document type is displayed in the Manager reports, and can be used to select chapters in Query mode.

Keywords: You can enter up to three keywords. The keywords are used to select chapters in Query mode. Note that these three fields will not accept lower-case letters; they are converted to upper-case.

Size: This field displays page size. It displays in inches, regardless of which unit of measurement used to specify the page.

Orientation: This field shows the orientation of the page (Portrait or Landscape).

Pages: This field displays the number of pages in the chapter.

File Data Subfunction

The File Data subfunction provides detailed information on a chapter's component files. It is invoked by clicking on the File button at the bottom of the Chapter Information dialog box (refer to Figure 4-5).

The File Data subfunction has two display modes. The default mode is File Name, which displays the full path specification of each component file (Figure 4-6). The second mode is File Info, which displays the filename, file type (such as, Chapter, Text, Line Art), time, date, and size of each component file (Figure 4-7).

You can switch between the two display modes by clicking on the File Name or File Info buttons located in the lower left of each dialog box. When you are done reviewing the information, click Done. You return to the Chapter Information dialog box.

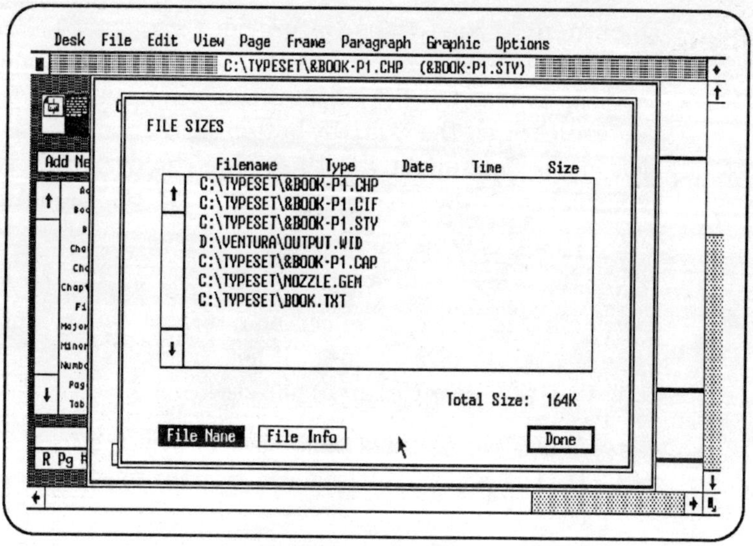

Figure 4-6

The File Data subfunction displays up to ten files at a time. If the chapter file contains more than ten files, use the arrows, or slider bar next to the file list to display additional files.

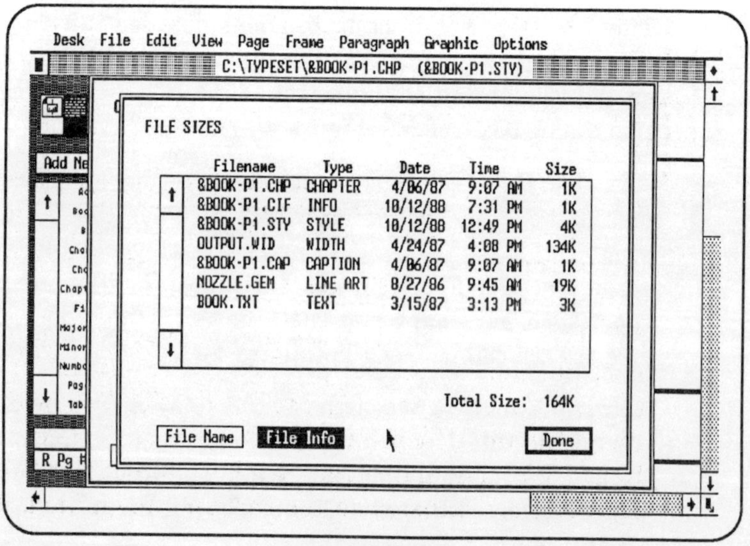

Figure 4-7

Chapter History Subfunction

The Chapter History subfunction provides a record of events for a given chapter. It is invoked by clicking the History button at the bottom of the Chapter Information dialog box (refer to Figure 4-5).

The Chapter History dialog box shown in Figure 4-8 is displayed. When the chapter file is created or the chapter revision rolled, Manager makes an entry into the chapter history. If the chapter was created before Manager was installed, the Operator ID field is blank. Otherwise, the ID field shows the initials of the person using Ventura (or Manager) at the time.

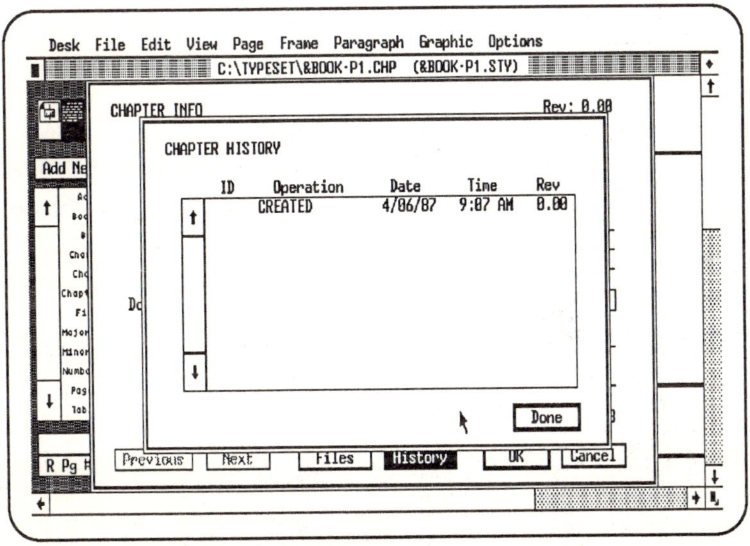

Figure 4-8

An entry is also made each time a chapter is printed. Keep in mind that Manager has no way to tell if you selected Cancel in the Ventura Print dialog box, or in the Item Selector if a print-to-disk operation is underway. Hence, you may find entries displayed which don't really represent occasions when the chapter was printed. Also,

Xerox Ventura Publisher Multi-Chapter prints are not recorded under Xerox Ventura Publisher version 1.1.

Chapter saves are also recorded provided you used the file menu. If you used the shortcut Ctrl-S instead, no entry is made. This lets you determine whether or not to keep a record based on the method you use to save.

Each event is recorded with the operator's ID, time, date, and current chapter revision level (Figure 4-8). The last 31 events are maintained in the chapter information file. Additional events overwrite the earliest entry. For example, the first entry in the history data is generated when the file is created. When the 32nd entry is generated, the creation entry is discarded.

Style Sheet Information

The Information function operates differently if you select it in Style Sheet mode. Instead of displaying information about a chapter, it displays the names and parameters of each tag in the active style sheet (Figure 4-9).

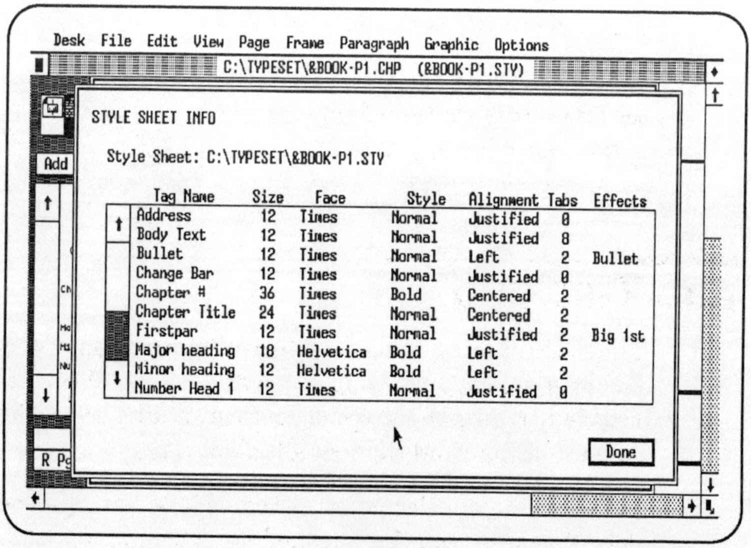

Figure 4-9

Tag information is displayed in seven fields. These fields are described below:

Tag Name: The name of the tag from the style sheet.

Size: The point size of the text.

Face: The name of the typeface. Note that Swiss will be displayed as Times and Dutch will be listed as Helvetica. These names are derived from the official published list of Face IDs for Xerox Ventura Publisher. If you have installed additional fonts which are not in that list, this field will be blank, or contain an incorrect description.

Style: Indicates the style of the text — Normal, Italic, Bold, and Bold Italic.

Alignment: Indicates whether the tag is left or right aligned, justified, centered or decimal aligned.

Tabs: Indicates the number of active tabs.

Effects: This field lists any special effects selected for this tag. The word "Bullet" will be displayed for a bullet item, and "Big" for big first character. If the field is blank, this tag has no special effects.

Up to ten tags may be displayed at a time. If more than ten tags are contained in the style sheet, use the up arrow, down arrow, or slider box next to display additional entries.

Job Tracking

The Job Tracking function follows the progress of a chapter or publication. (It is not valid in the Style Sheet mode.) It tracks the stage of completion, the schedule, the current status, and the individuals involved.

Once you have selected an active chapter or publication, Job Tracking can be invoked by clicking on the Job

Tracking button in the main dialog box. The Job Tracking dialog box appears (Figure 4-10).

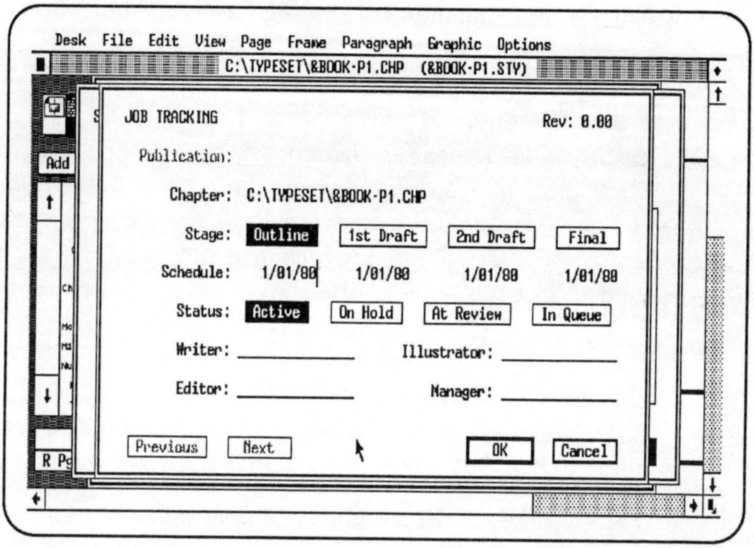

Figure 4-10

Job Tracking Fields

The Job Tracking dialog box contains the fields described below.

Publication: The file specification for the active publication. If you are in Chapter mode, the label is disabled, and the field is blank.

Chapter: The name of the current chapter.

Stage: Four buttons that indicate stage of completion.

Schedule: A schedule date for each of the four job stages.

Status: Four buttons to indicate the current status of the active chapter.

Writer: The name of the writer.

Illustrator: The name of the individual responsible for generating graphics.

Editor: The name of the editor.

Manager: The name of the individual with overall responsibility for the document.

You can move between these fields using the Tab key, or the mouse.

Report/Query

The report subfunction lets you print a report containing data from a chapters' information file. It is invoked by clicking on the Report/Query button at the bottom of the main dialog box. The Report/Query dialog box appears (Figure 4-11).

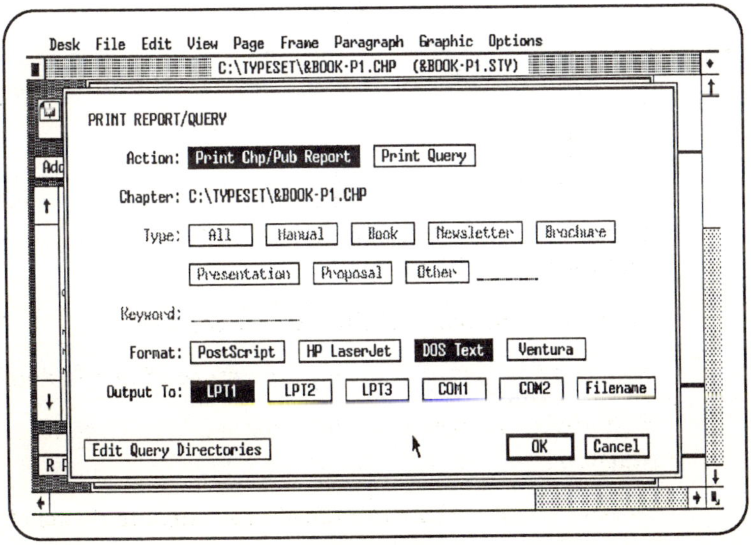

Figure4-11

The top two buttons in this dialog box select the Report or Query mode. Report mode produces a report for the active chapter or publication. Query mode prints the same report, but only for those chapters matching the document type and keyword you specify. You can specify up to ten directories where you want Manager to look for chapters in Query mode.

Printing a Chapter/Pub Report

In Report mode, Manager displays the active chapter or publication in the field directly below the top two buttons. If you are in the Chapter mode, a report is printed about that chapter. In the publication mode, the same report is repeated for each chapter in the publication.

The Format buttons select the report format. PostScript, HP LaserJet, DOS text file (ASCII), or Ventura file. These formats are described fully in Appendix A. You can modify or customize them to produce different report layouts, and contents.

To print a report select the output format in which you wish the report to be printed.

☞ *NOTE: In PostScript, HP LaserJet, and DOS text format, you can send a report directly to a printer without exiting Manager or Ventura.*

The Output To line controls the destination of the report. You can select one of the parallel ports, serial ports, or have the report printed to a file. If you select Filename, the Item Selector will display once you click on the OK button. You can then enter the filename.

If you select Ventura as the output format, the destination is automatically set to Filename. Once the report has been printed to a file, you can load it into a Xerox Ventura Publisher chapter to format, edit, and print.

Printing a Query

If you select Query mode, Manager enables the Document Type and Keyword selections. The Document Type buttons and Keyword fields let you selectively print reports for certain chapters. You select the document type by selecting one of the buttons.

If you select the All button, the document type is ignored. If you select one of the predefined buttons, the chapter must match the predefined document type to be printed. If the Other type button is selected, the chapter must also be Other type, and the user-definable types must match. However, if you leave the user-definable field blank, Manager accepts all chapters with a document type of Other, regardless of what user-definable type is specified.

The keywords work in a similar manner. Each chapter can have up to three keywords. If you enter a keyword in the Keyword field, only chapters with a matching keyword are accepted. If you leave the Keyword field blank, all chapters are accepted regardless of what keyword(s) they contain.

The Document Type and Keyword selectors work together. If you select a document type (other than All), and a keyword, *the chapter must match both criteria to be printed.* For example if the document type is Manual, and the Keywords are USER'S GUIDE, only those chapters with a document type of Manual, and USER'S GUIDE as two of their three keywords are accepted. If you want all chapters printed, select All for the document type, and leave the Keyword field blank.

To print a Query report, you *must* specify which directories Manager should search for. Do this by clicking on the Edit Query Directories button at the bottom of the dialog box. The dialog box in Figure 4-12 displays.

You add directories by clicking on the Add Directory button in the lower left-hand corner. The Item Selector displays, so you can select a directory. You can select additional directories to a maximum of ten.

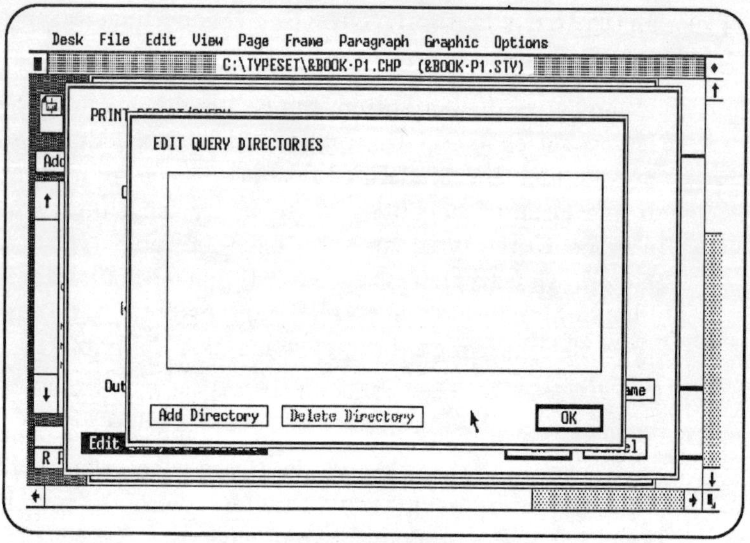

Figure 4-12

You can delete a directory by clicking on the directory entry you wish to delete. Manager displays the selected directory in reverse video. Once you have selected the entry, the Delete Directory button is enabled. Delete the entry by clicking the button. You can deselect an entry by clicking it a second time, or clicking on another entry. When you are done, click OK.

☞ *NOTE: If you fail to add any chapters, the Query function will not work properly. Manager will not know where to look for the chapters you want.*

The format and destination of a Query report is selected in the same manner as the chapter and publication reports described above.

Timed Backup

The Timed Backup function automatically saves the chapter you are working on at specified intervals. This helps preserve your valuable data from system and software mishaps.

Timed Backup Operation

Manager maintains an internal clock to determine when timed backup should take place. The default interval is 5 minutes, but you can also specify intervals of 10, 15, or 30 minutes. The system speaker will sound 30 seconds *before* each backup takes place. If this is the first interval for the chapter you are working on, the dialog box shown in Figure 4-13 displays.

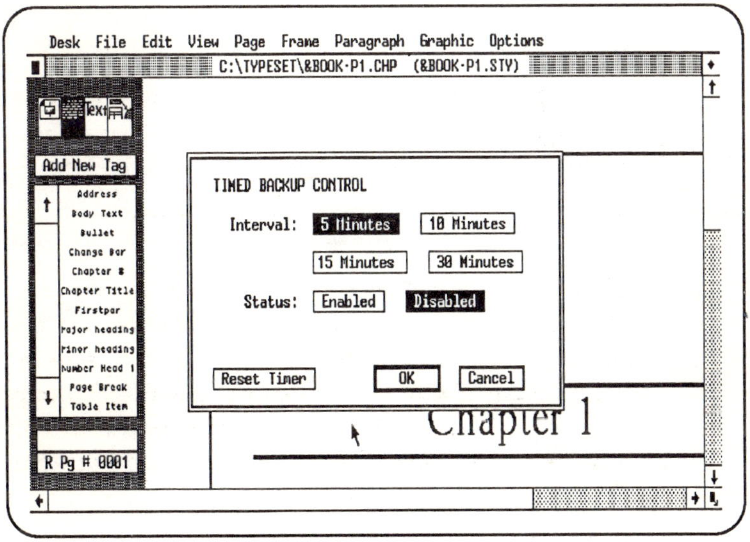

Figure 4-13

If you want timed backup for the current chapter, click Enabled, click OK. The chapter will automatically be saved 30 seconds later. The speaker will beep 30 seconds before the end of each subsequent interval, but the dialog box will not be displayed (unless a new chapter is opened).

Timed Backup saves are not entered into the chapter history. A Timed Backup will not occur while you are in the middle of a Xerox Ventura Publisher dialog box, or while any of the Xerox Ventura Publisher menus are pulled down.

If you don't wish to periodically save the current chapter, you may disable the Timed Backup feature. Select the Timed Backup mode by entering an Alt-T. The dialog box shown in Figure 4-13 displays. Select the Disabled button, then click OK.

Temporarily Disabling Timed Backup

The 30-second warning provides you with the opportunity of temporarily disabling the timed backup. You can reset the timer at any time, effectively disabling backup for that one interval.

There are several instances where you may wish to disable the Timed Backup function. If you are modifying an existing style sheet in preparation for creating a new one, you do not want a backup to take place, as the source style sheet contents will be modified. Of course, you can do a Save As Diff. Style before you make any modifications, so that when a timed backup occurs, the source style sheet will not be modified.

To reset the backup timer, press Alt-T. Click on the Reset Timer button, then click OK. The internal timer will be reset, effectively disabling the timed backup until the next interval.

Changing the Timed Backup Interval

You can change the interval between backups to suit your needs. Select the Timed Backup mode by pressing Alt-T. The dialog box in Figure 4-13 displays.

Four backup intervals are supported by the program; 5, 10, 15, or 30 minutes. The amount of time between backups can be selected by clicking on the appropriate button in the dialog box. Once you have made your selections, click OK, or Cancel to restore the previous parameters.

File Management

The File Management mode is selected using Alt-F. The dialog box in Figure 4-14 displays. It provides you with the ability to manage files, chapters, publications, directories, and style sheets.

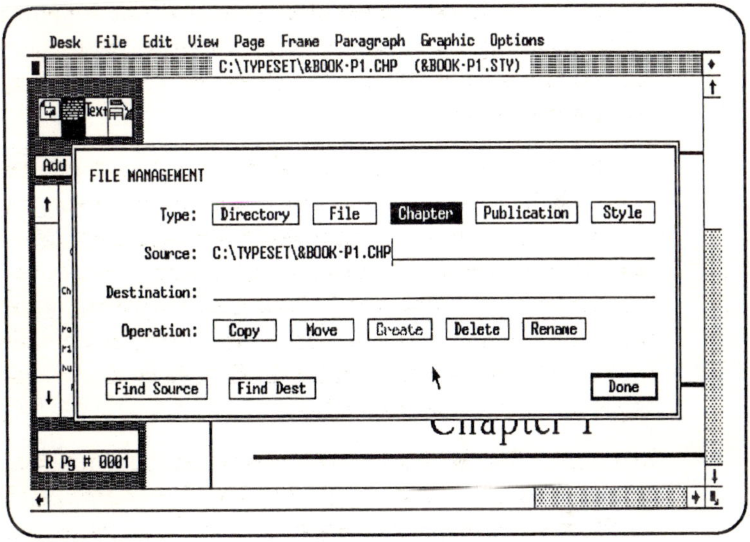

Figure 4-14

Manager needs four pieces of information for most file management functions. First, you must specify the type of file — a directory, a DOS file, Ventura chapter, publication, or a style sheet. Next, you must specify a source file name, and (in most cases), a destination filename. Finally, you must indicate the operation you want (such as, Copy, Move).

Selecting a Source and Destination

Each file operation must have a source filename. For example, to copy a chapter from one directory to another, the source is the chapter name, including the full path.

You can type in the source directly, or click on the Find Source button in the lower left-hand corner. Manager then displays the Item Selector so that you can select the file. Manager maintains a starting directory and file filter for each type of file.

You select a destination file in the same manner. You can type the filename, or click on the Find Dest button.

For some operations, the destination is not a file, but a directory. All directories names *must* end with the backslash "\" character. For example,

```
C:\TYPESET
```

is incorrect, while

```
C:\TYPESET\
```

will be accepted.

Directory Operations

You can create and delete directories in Manager. Select the Directory button in the Type: field. To add a directory to one of the disk drives, enter the name of the new directory into the Source field, or select it with the Find Source button. Specifying a directory to create is the one exception to normal naming conventions. *Do not put the backslash character (\) on the end.* (This is to conform with DOS conventions which do not use this character with the MKDIR command).

You can delete unwanted directories in a similar manner. Type the name of the directory in the Source field, or select it using Find Source. Note that the directory name must end with the backslash character (\). Remember that a directory must be empty before it can be deleted. Click the Delete button to remove the directory.

File Operations

Manager provides a complete set of file operations to copy, move, delete, and rename files from within Ventura. This feature is particularly helpful in managing the myriad files which make up Ventura chapters and publications.

☞ *Although the file management features of Manager are available without exiting Ventura, it is strongly recommended that you DO NOT copy, move, delete, or rename any of the component files of the currently open chapter.*

Manager's copy and move operations are very similar. The copy operation makes a copy of the specified file in the destination directory. The move operation makes a copy of the specified file, then deletes the original.

To initiate either operation, select the File button, then enter the source filename, either directly in Source field, or using the Find Source button. Manager supports the standard DOS wildcards "?" and "*" to select multiple files, or individual file names.

Next, specify the destination directory. As with the source file name, you can select the destination by typing it in the Destination field, or via the Find Dest button.

Once you have specified the source and destination, click on Copy or Move. Manager copies or moves the file(s) into the destination directory.

Before Manager copies a file, it checks to see if the file already exits. If it does, the warning message shown in Figure 4-15 is displayed. The name, time, and date of both the source and destination files are displayed. You can either copy over the old file with the Overwrite button, or keep it with Keep Old. You should note that this warning message is displayed every time there is a file duplication, even if the time and date of the two files match, which is usually a good indication that the files are identical.

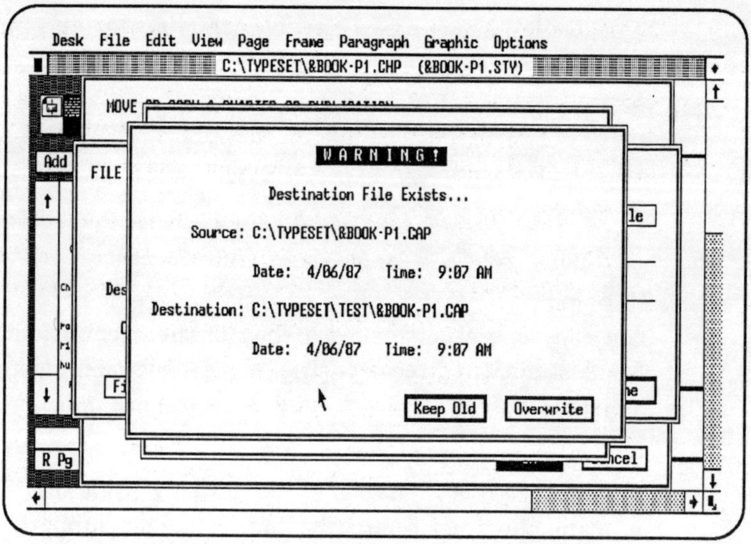

Figure 4-15

The delete file operation lets you delete files from your disk drive. Select the File button, then enter the name of the file(s) to delete. Multiple files can be specified using the DOS wildcard characters "?" and "*". Finally, click on the Delete button. Manager asks you to confirm that you wish to delete the file(s).

Rename is the final operation. Manager lets you rename any file in your system. Like other file operations, the File button must be selected. Type the source directly in the Source field or select it using the Find Source button. Likewise, you must enter the destination filename in the Destination field. You can use the DOS wildcard characters. Once you have selected the source and destination, click the Rename button.

Chapter and Publication Operations

The chapter and publication operations are virtually identical to those for files. Manager lets you copy, move, delete, and rename Ventura chapters and publications. You have control over which component files are moved, and which stay behind. Like the Xerox Ventura Publisher

Multi-Chapter operations, the Manager chapter and publication operations provide the means to use existing chapters as the basis for new chapters, create archive copies of important documents, and organize your library of Ventura documents as it grows over time.

☞ *NOTE: When Manager copies or moves a chapter or publication, it automatically changes the file pointers in the chapter file(s) so Ventura can find the component files in their new location.*

First select a chapter or publication by clicking on the appropriate button. Then, select a chapter(s) or publication(s) by typing the name into the Source field, or by clicking on the Find Source button. As with file operations, the DOS wildcard characters "?" and "*" can be included to specify more than one chapter or publication.

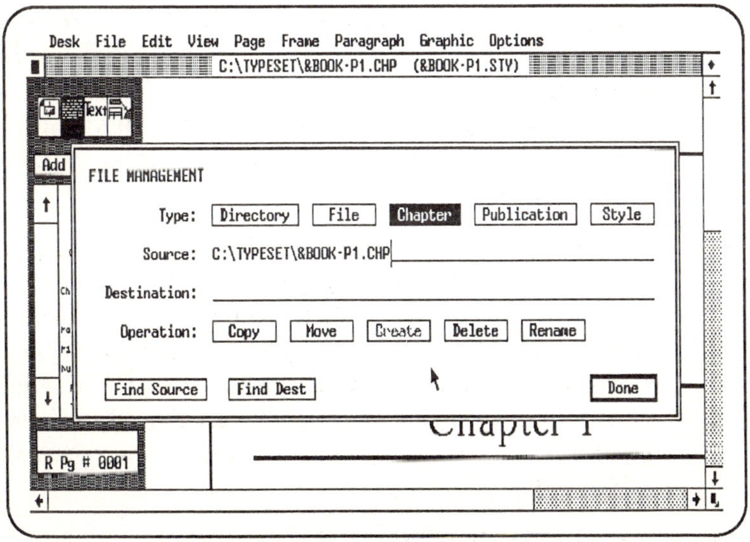

Figure 4-16

Select the destination directory by typing it into the Destination field, or by clicking on the Dest button.

Once you have selected the file type, the source and the destination, click on Copy or Move. Manager displays the screen in Figure 4-17.

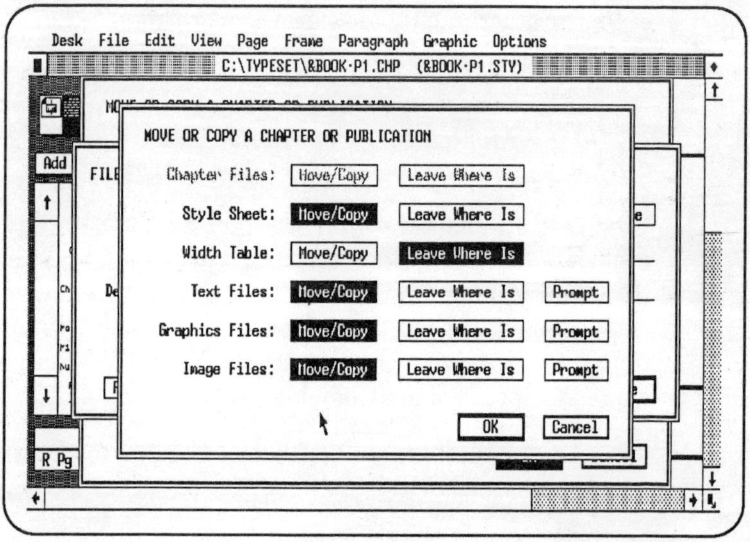

Figure 4-17

Manager can move all or any part of a chapter or publication. In Chapter mode, you can specify if the style sheet and width table are to be moved. Excluding the style sheet from the copy or move operation lets you use the same style sheet for multiple documents. Likewise, the ability to leave the Ventura width table in its current location (usually the \VENTURA directory) prevents multiple copies of a width table from being scattered around your hard disk drive.

In Publication mode, the Chapter buttons are enabled, and you can specify if you want the .CHP, .CAP, .VGR, and .CIF files moved or not.

In both modes, you can specify whether text, graphic and image files are to be moved, left in place. In addition, you can ask Manager to prompt you for each file so you can decide on a case-by-case basis.

Once you've set these options to your satisfaction, click OK. Manager displays the screen shown in Figure 4-18. Each file type can be moved to a separate directory.

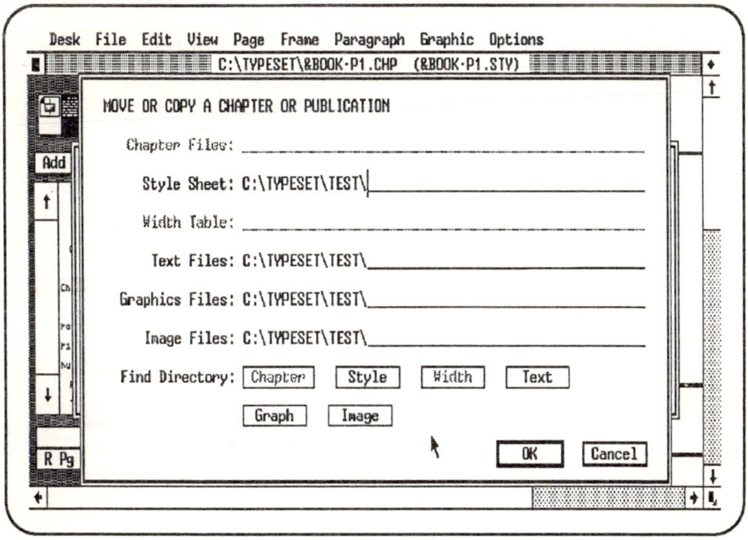

Figure 4-18

Initially, all of these directories are set to the directory you specified in the Destination field, but you can change any or all of them. You can type directories directly, or click on the appropriate button at the bottom of the dialog box and select the directory with the Item Selector. When you have set the directories as desired, click OK.

Before Manager copies a chapter or publication into a directory, it checks to make sure it doesn't already exist. If it does, a warning screen is displayed so you can resolve the file conflict.

Style Sheet Operations

Style sheet operations are essentially identical to the file operations discussed earlier. The directory of the active style sheet is displayed each time a style sheet operation is selected. The copy, move, delete, and rename functions work the same as their corresponding file operation.

☞ *WARNING: Take care when performing style sheet operations. In many cases, more than one chapter will use the same style sheet. Before you move, delete, or rename a style sheet, make sure that it is not used by any chapter on your system, otherwise that chapter will not be formatted correctly the next time it is opened.*

Appendix A

Manager Reports

This Appendix provides you with the information to modify or customize Manager reports.

It is not necessary for you to master the material in this appendix unless you wish to alter Manager's standard report format.

Manager Report Files

Manager generates reports with (1) a source file and (2) information from the chapter information file(s). There is a separate source file for each of the three printer types supported, PostScript, HP LaserJet, and DOS text. A fourth source file lets you to select a Ventura file format which can be read into a Ventura chapter. These source files contain the bulk of the data sent to the printer, and they determine the format of the report. You can customize your reports by altering the contents of these source files.

Literal Characters

Report files consist of *literal characters* and *tokens*. Literal characters are sent verbatim to the printer (or printer file if Filename output has been selected). A Literal character can be any character value from 0 to 255 (8 bits). They are not limited to ASCII or any other range, unless required by the printer (for instance, PostScript characters must be almost exclusively ASCII characters).

Literal characters are used for titles, headings, separators, Carriage Return/Line Feed, Form Feed, and other functions. All Literal characters are output, unmodified, to the printer or printer file.

Tokens

Tokens insert chapter information into a report. Each token consists of the ASCII ampersand character (&) followed by a two digit ASCII number. &09 is an example of a valid Manager report token. Each token corresponds to a specific data item from the chapter information file. Table A-1 shows the correlation between tokens and data.

Whenever Manager encounters a token in the print file, it replaces the token with its associated data. For example, if the print file contained the following characters

```
PUB: &04
```

the printed report will read

```
PUB: C:\TYPESET\&EXAMPLE.PUB
```

The token (&04) is replaced with the file specification of the current publication (C:\TYPESET\&EXAMPLE.PUB). All tokens are handled in a similar manner.

Although the ampersand character is used for tokens, it is possible to include this character in a report. A double ampersand (&&) is treated as an *escape* sequence, indicating that a literal ampersand is to be printed. Double ampersands may be printed by including successive escape sequences (&&&&) in the print file.

Component File Data

Most of the tokens described in Table A-1 are fairly straightforward. They represent one of the fields displayed in the Manager dialog boxes. However, the component file group merits some additional discussion.

A Xerox Ventura Publisher file can contain up to 128 component files. Component files consist of text, line art, and images, as well the Chapter files (.CHP, .CAP, .VGR,

Manager Tokens

&01–Current DOS time
&02–Current DOS date
&03–Publication file specification
&04–Chapter file specification
&05–Style Sheet file specification
&06–Width Table file specification
&07–Chapter description field #1
&08–Chapter description field #2
&09–Chapter description field #3
&10–Publication revision
&11–Chapter major revision
&12–Chapter minor revision
&13–Revision current indication
&14–Last revision date
&15–Last revision time
&16–Date chapter was last printed
&17–Time chapter was last printed
&18–Date chapter was archived
&19–Time chapter was archived
&20–Date chapter was created
&21–Time chapter was created
&22–Completion stage of chapter
&23–Outline schedule date
&24–1st Draft schedule date
&25–2nd Draft schedule date
&26–Final Draft schedule date
&27–Chapter status
&28–Writer
&29–Illustrator
&30–Editor
&31–Manager
&32 Component file specification
&33–Component file type
&34–Component file date
&35–Component file time
&36–Component file size
&37–Start component file loop
&38–End component file loop
&39–Not Used
&40–Form feed

Table A-1

and .CIF). You have no way of knowing when you construct a report file how many component files will be contained in any given chapter file. The component file group of tokens was designed to simplify the task of including component file data in reports.

Simply stated, a component file group consists of a Start of Group token (&37) followed by literal text and tokens, and terminated by an End of Group token (&38). These components of the report source file interact as follows.

When a Start of Group token is encountered, the position of the next character is saved. The file is then parsed in the normal manner until an End of Group token is encountered. The position of the first character after the End of Group token is also saved.

Manager will then return to the first character following the Start of Group token, effectively creating a loop. The characters between the Start of Group and End of Group tokens will be parsed again.

Whenever the Start of Group and End of Group tokens are utilized, the Component file specification token (&32) must be included in the file between them. The Component file specification token will exit the loop and instruct Manager to resume parsing after the End of Group token when there are no more component files to be displayed. In addition, this token advances the internal component file pointer to the next file, so that the other component file tokens (type, date, time, size) will display data for all of the component files in a chapter.

☞ *Failure to include the Component file specification token between Start of Group and End of Group tokens will result in Manager entering an endless loop.*

Printer Types

Manager supports three printer types, PostScript, HP LaserJet, and DOS text printers, plus a Ventura file format. Each printer type has a different source file in the VENTURA subdirectory. These files are POSTSCPT.PRT, HPLASJET.PRT, DOS_TEXT.PRT, and VENTURA.PRT.

The POSTSCPT.PRT file contains a PostScript program which prints the standard Manager report format. If you wish to modify the source file, you should be reasonably familiar with PostScript programming. The program is not a terribly complex one, but you should be familiar with PostScript basics before attempting to modify it.

The HPLASJET.PRT file is intended for use with HP LaserJet printers, and printers which emulate the HP PCL command set. To ensure maximum compatibility with the HP LaserJet series of printers, the source file included with Manager consists of ASCII characters and tokens. No attempt has been made to utilize cartridge or downloadable fonts. If you wish to enhance the format of this report format, you may add HP PCL commands and escape sequences to the file.

The final file is the DOS_TEXT.PRT file. This file contains ASCII characters and tokens, and is intended to printed on non-PostScript and non-HP Laserjet printers, such as the Epson MX, RX, FX-80 series and compatibles.

The Ventura file creates a pre-tagged report which can be read into Xerox Ventura Publisher. The report is tagged for use with the REPORT.STY style sheet which was installed in the TYPESET directory when Desktop Manager was installed. The file should be read into Xerox Ventura Publisher as a Generated file with the Load Text/File dialog box.

NOTES

NOTES

NOTES

Appendix B

Installation Notes

Manager requires approximately 8K of system memory to run. In a normal environment (DOS 3.x, a mouse driver, and Xerox Ventura Publisher) there is approximately 130K to 150K of free memory in Ventura before VP Manager is installed. Thus the little over 8K occupied by Manager is not particularly noticeable.

Manager consists of six program files:

- MANAGER.APP
- MANAGER.RSC
- MANAGER1.OVR
- MANAGER1.RSC
- MANGER2.OVR
- MANAGER2.RSC.

The MANAGER.APP file is responsible for loading the other files as needed. These program must reside in the same directory as the Xerox Ventura Publisher program files. In most installations this will be the \VENTURA directory. In addition to the program files, the four report template files POSTSCPT.PRT, HPLASJET.PRT, DOS_TEXT.PRT, and VENTURA.PRT must also reside in this directory.

The installation program finds the batch file which starts Ventura, copies it as VPMAN.BAT and replaces the parameter VP in the line beginning with DRVRMRGR with the parameter MANAGER. Here is a sample batch file after Manager has been installed:

```
CD \VENTURA
DRVRMRGR MANAGER %1 /S=SD_HERC5.EGA/M=32
```

You can run Ventura without Manager at ay time by typing the normal Ventura command (VP for Ventura 1.1 or Ventura 2, and VPPROF for the Professional Extension). To run Ventura together with Manager, type VPMAN.

If You Have Changed or Relocated the Startup Batch File

Some advanced users modify and/or relocate the batch file that starts up Ventura. Manager's installation program expects to find this batch file in the root directory where it is left by the Ventura installation program.

If you have moved the batch file to a different subdirectory, Manager will not be able to find it. Installation will fail. To install Manager, copy the batch file back to the root directory (VP.BAT for Ventura 1.1 and VPPROF.BAT for the Professional Extension). Then install Manager again. This time Manager will be able to find the file and, therefore, to create its own VPMAN.BAT startup file.

After installation, you can relocate the original batch file and the new VPMAN.BAT file as you see fit.

If you have created different versions of the startup batch files, you should decide which one you want to use as the starting point for the VPMAN batch file. Temporarily copy that file to the root directory as VP.BAT. Then install Manager. When finished with installation, you can remove the temporary VP.BAT file.

Advanced users can create multiple Manager batch files by modifying their current Ventura batch files. Simply substitute the word "MANAGER" in place of the word "VP" (or VPPROF if you are using the Professional Extension).

NOTES

NOTES

Appendix C

Manager and Memory

Xerox Ventura Publisher is one of the most robust applications ever written for the IBM PC. It pushes the technology to the limits. One of the limits it tests the most often is the 640K memory restriction of DOS. When Ventura runs out of RAM, it may slow down, or even refuse to load complex chapters.

Desktop Manager uses about 8K of memory over and above what is taken by Ventura. That's not very much. Nevertheless, there may be occasional complex documents that you might have a problem loading.

This appendix presents some solutions to memory problems. If you are not having memory difficulties, you do not need to take any steps. However, if you occasionally experience error messages, try some of the ideas below. (Incidentally, most of these strategies are valuable even for someone who uses Ventura without Manager.)

In order of preference, here are the steps you can take:

- use expanded memory
- upgrade to the Professional Extension
- make your documents shorter and less complex
- free up more system memory
- use Ventura alone (without Manager) for extremely complex documents

Let's consider each option briefly.

Adding Expanded Memory

If there's expanded memory available, Ventura Version 2 can use it to store certain program overlays, thereby speeding operation. Better yet, the Professional Extension can use expanded memory for building documents, thereby eliminating many memory problems.

Upgrading to Professional Extension

Because of its use of expanded memory, the Professional Extension removes some of the memory limitations that apply to Ventura Version 2. You may be able to overcome your problems by upgrading.

Making Documents Shorter and Less Complex

You may be able to circumvent memory problems with two simple strategies. First, avoid memory-hungry page elements. Second, break documents into smaller pieces.

Certain page elements eat into available memory. In particular, tabs, tags, and leader dots are memory hungry. Therefore:

- Eliminate unneeded tags from your style sheet since they consume memory whether used or not.
- Use Body Text for the most common page element. You cannot eliminate the Body Text tag, so make good use of it. Each time you add a tag you consume more memory. You can minimize additional tags by assigning Body Text to the most common page element.
- Use line breaks instead of paragraphs, particularly for documents such as directories with many paragraphs per page. Wherever possible, start new lines with a line break instead of a carriage return to preserve memory.
- Take memory from the screen buffer and add it to the text area. Add the /A switch to the end of the VPMAN.BAT file. This switch transfers screen

(graphics) memory to text, so you can build longer documents before spooling becomes necessary. However, you so pay a penalty, since you are stealing memory used to display and convert pictures. In fact, some printers and conversions won't work without the full screen buffer. You can specify any amount in 1K increments up to a maximum of 32. For instance, if you transfer 15K to text, you have effectively canceled out the 15K Manager uses. Here's how it would look in a typical VPMAN.BAT batch file:

```
DRVRMRGR MANAGER %1 /S=SD_VGA_5.VGA/M=01/A=15
```

- Consider limiting Ventura documents to thirty pages or less. The simplest way to overcome memory problems in a long chapter is to split it into two parts. Then you can relink when you print, by printing through the Multi-Chapter dialog box, and specifying automatic numbering across chapter boundaries.

Freeing More RAM

If you don't have the budget to add expanded memory and/or the Professional Extension, try taking steps to maximize the amount of memory available to Ventura. Here are some ways to free up RAM:

- Do not use any memory resident applications together with Manager and Ventura. This includes DOS shells, print spoolers, and desk accessories.
- Eliminate device drivers from the CONFIG.SYS file unless they are absolutely necessary.
- Reduce the buffers to 15 (Substitute "BUFFERS=15" for the current buffers command in the CONFIG.SYS file).
- Use only one hyphenation algorithm.
- Reduce the size of the user hyphenation dictionary if it has more than a few words in it.

- Consider switching to an older version of DOS, which uses less RAM than your current version. For instance, DOS 3.0 uses about 15K more than DOS 2.0. Likewise, an EGA board consumes slightly more system memory than a Hercules card.
- You may be able to increase memory to 704K if you have an extended memory board such as the JLaser Plus AT board. The JLaser board can allocate an additional 64K of memory to DOS. Xerox Ventura Publisher will recognize this additional memory. Insert this command into the CONFIG.SYS file:

```
DEVICE=JBOOT.BIN 704K
```

☞ *NOTE: The JLaser printer driver uses less than 10K, compared to as much as 30K or more for a PostScript driver. When this extra 20K is combined with the additional 64K of DOS Memory, the JLaser board makes an extra 84K available to Xerox Ventura Publisher — a substantial amount.*

Using Ventura Alone

We caution you against this last option except as a last resort. You can't take advantage of Manager's convenience and safety features if it isn't loaded. What's more, many of Manager's job tracking functions are predicated on knowing which operator performed which task. To track the operator's initials, you must have Manager loaded together with Ventura.

☞ *NOTE: If you can't load a document with Manager resident, that document is probably very close to being too complex even without Manager. In other words, if you have memory problems with Manager, you're probably going to have them without it as well. Your best bet is to take immediate steps to improve the situation.*

However, if you want to run Ventura alone, it is quite simple. Type VP from the DOS prompt (VPPROF if you have the Professional Extension). Ventura will load without Manager. To use Ventura together with Desktop Manager again, type VPMAN from the DOS prompt.

☞ *TIP: You don't have to open a chapter to work on it with Manager. Even if a document is too complex to load, you can still perform all of Manager's file and document management functions on that chapter. Just don't try to load it.*

NOTES

Index

S

T

U

DESKTOP MANAGER

ISBN: 0-934035-34-2 **$99.95**
Supports Version 1 and 2

Desktop Manager is the desktop accessory software for IBM and compatible personal computers that helps your manage your Ventura Publisher documents, running transparently from within the Ventura Publisher environment. A multifunction software utility, *Desktop Manager* provides file management, timed backup, document control, style sheet settings, and report generation. This essential utility program comes complete with an 180-page guide.

STYLE SHEETS FOR BUSINESS DOCUMENTS

(Book and Disk Set)
Martha Lubow and Jesse Berst
320 pages, 150 illustrations
ISBN 0-934035-22-9 **$39.95**
Supports Version 1 and 2

Introducing a cure for the common document—*Style Sheets for Business Documents*. This book and disk set contains more than 30 predesigned Ventura Publisher templates for creating top-quality business documents. Style sheets are presented for proposals, reports, marketing materials, ads, brochures, and correspondence. More than 100 pages of design tips and tricks are also included.

STYLE SHEETS FOR TECHNICAL DOCUMENTS

(Book and Disk Set)
By Byron Canfield and Chad Canty
320 Pages 150 illustrations
ISBN: 0-934035-29-6 **$39.95**
Supports Version 1 and 2

Get the maximum out of Ventura Publisher with these advanced technical document formats. This book/disk combination presents more than 25 ready-to-use templates for creating technical documents and books. Also includes techniques for creating pictures and tables, plus advanced tips for modifying formats to fit your needs.

STYLE SHEETS FOR NEWSLETTERS

(Book and Disk Set)
By Martha Lubow and Polly Pattison
320 Pages over 150 illustrations
ISBN: 0-934035-31-8 **$39.95**
Supports Version 1 and 2

This book and disk set presents more than 25 predesigned Ventura Publisher templates for creating one-, two-, three-, and four-column newsletters. Just open the chapter template, load in your own text, and print. A complete description of every style sheet and key tag for all chapter templates is also included.

NEW WRITING

By Jesse Berst
320 Pages over 150 illustrations
ISBN: 0-934035-27-X **$9.95**

The essential handbook for the modern writer and editor. *New Writing* shows you how to save production time by preformatting documents. Learn to manage your files, styles and style sheets. Also presented are the elements of style you need to succeed in today's desktop publishing arena. Companion software is available.

New Riders Library also includes books on AutoCAD

INSIDE AUTOCAD

D. Raker and H. Rice
750 pages, over 400 illustrations
ISBN: 0-934035-49-0 **$29.95**

INSIDE AutoCAD, the best selling book on AutoCAD, is entirely new and rewritten for AutoCAD's 3D Release 10. This easy-to-understand book serves as both a tutorial and a lasting reference guide.

INSIDE AUTOLISP

J. Smith and R. Gesner
672 pages, over 150 illustrations
ISBN: 0-934035-47-4 **$29.95**

Introducing the most comprehensive book on AutoLISP for AutoCAD Release 10. Learn AutoLISP commands and functions and write your own custom AutoLISP programs.

INSIDE AUTOSKETCH

By Frank Lenk
240 pages, over 120 illustrations
ISBN: 0-934035-20-2 **$17.95**

INSIDE AutoSketch gives you real-life mechanical parts, drawing schematics, and architectural drawings.

CUSTOMIZING AUTOCAD

J. Smith and R. Gesner
480 pages, over 100 illustrations
ISBN: 0-934035-45-8 **$27.95**

Uncover the hidden secrets of AutoCAD's 3D Release 10 in this all new edition. Discover the anatomy of an AutoCAD menu and build a custom menu from start to finish.

AUTOCAD FOR ARCHITECTS AND ENGINEERS

John Albright and Elizabeth Schaeffer
480 pages, over 160 illustrations
ISBN: 0-934035-53-9 **$29.95**

Learn by doing a typical AEC project using high-powered design development with AutoCAD Release 10. Learn to construct working drawings using techniques from real life AEC projects.

STEPPING INTO AUTOCAD

By Mark Merickel
380 pages, over 140 illustrations
ISBN: 0-934035-51-2 **$29.95**

This popular tutorial has been completely rewritten with new exercises for Release 10. The book is organized to lead you step by step from the basics to practical tips on customizing AutoCAD for technical drafting.

AUTOCAD QUICK REFERENCE GUIDE
New Riders Publishing
180 pages, over 50 illustrations
ISBN: 0-934035-57-1 **$11.95**

All essential AutoCAD functions and commands are arranged alphabetically and described in just a few paragraphs.

THE AUTODESK FILE
Written and Edited by John Walker
608 pages
ISBN 0-934035-63-6 **$24.95**

The unvarnished history of Autodesk, Inc. the company behind AutoCAD. Read the original memos, letters and reports that trace the rise of Autodesk, from start-up to their present position as the number one CAD software company in the world.

NEW RIDERS LICENSE STATEMENT

This software is protected by both United States copyright law and international treaty provisions. Therefore; you must treat this software just like a book, with the following single exception. New Riders Publishing authorizes you to make archival copies of the software for the sole purpose of backing-up our software and protecting your investment from loss.

By saying "just like a book," New Riders Publishing means, for example, that this software may be used by any number of people and may be freely moved from one computer location to another, so long as there is NO possibility of it being used at one location while it's being used at another. Just like a book that can't be read by two different people in two different places at the same time, neither can the software be used by two different people in two different places at the same time.

LIMITED WARRANTY

With respect to the physical diskette and physical documentation enclosed herein, New Riders Publishing warrants the same to be free of defects in materials and workmanship for a period of 90 days from the date of purchase. In the event of notification within the warranty period of defects in material or workmanship, New Riders will replace the defective diskette or documentation. **If you need to return a product, call the New Riders Publishing Customer Service Department to obtain a return authorization number.** The remedy for breach of the warranty shall be limited to replacement and shall not encompass any other damages, including but not limited to loss of profit, and special, incidental, consequential, or other similar claims.

New Riders Publishing specifically disclaims all other warranties, expressed or implied, including but not limited to implied warranties of merchantability and fitness for a particular purpose with respect to defects in the diskette and documentation, and the program license granted herein in particular, and without limiting operation of the program license with respect to any particular application, use, or purpose. In no event shall New Riders Publishing be liable for any loss of profit or any other commercial damage, including but not limited to special, incidental, consequential or other damages.

GOVERNING LAW

This statement shall be construed, interpreted, and governed by the laws of the state of New York.

DESKTOP MANAGER
WARRANTY REGISTRATION CARD

Name: ____

Company: ____

Address: ____

City: ____________________ State: _______ Zip: __________

Phone Number: _____________________________________

Date of Purchase: ________________________________

Dealer: ____

City: ____________________ State: _______ Zip: __________

Phone Number: _____________________________________

Comments: ____

____

____

Customer Survey — we would appreciate your input:

Number of employees in your company: _________________

Who purchased Desktop Manager: ❑ Company ❑ Self

Where will you use Desktop Manager: ❑ Home ❑ Office

Do you currently use any other New Riders products:

If yes, which ones: __________________________________

Would you like information on other New Riders products:

- ❑ Style Sheets for Xerox Ventura Publisher
- ❑ Style Sheet Manager for Xerox Ventura Publisher
- ❑ Inside Xerox Ventura Publisher
- ❑ Publishing Power with Ventura
- ❑ Inside Xerox Presents
- ❑ Inside Xerox Formbase
- ❑ Inside AutoCAD
- ❑ Inside AutoSketch

PLEASE FILL OUT AND MAIL THIS CARD BACK TODAY!

NO POSTAGE
NECESSARY
IF MAILED
IN THE
UNITED STATES

BUSINESS REPLY MAIL

FIRST CLASS PERMIT NO. 53 THOUSAND OAKS, CA

POSTAGE WILL BE PAID BY ADDRESSEE

New Riders Publishing
P.O. Box 4846
Thousand Oaks, CA 91359-9968

Order from New Riders Publishing Today

Name ______________________________

Company: ______________________________

Address: ______________________________

City: ______________________________

State ____________________ Zip: __________

Phone: ______________________________

- ❑ Check enclosed.
- ❑ Charge to my credit card:
- ❑ Visa # ______________________________
- ❑ Mastercard# ______________________________
- ❑ Expiration date: ______________________________
- ❑ Signature: ______________________________

Quantity	Description of Item	Unit Cost	Total Cost
	Inside Xerox Ventura Publisher 2nd Edition	$24.95	
	Publishing Power with Ventura 2nd Edition	$27.95	
	Publishing Power Disk	$14.95	
	Style Sheets for Business Documents–Book/Disk Set	$39.95	
	Style Sheets for Newsletters–Book/Disk Set	$39.95	
	Style Sheets for Technical Documents–Book/Disk Set	$39.95	
	New Writing	$ 9.95	
	New Writing – Desktop Utility Disk	$ 7.95	
	COOKIES (Put the fun back in your computer)	$ 6.95	
	Shipping and Handling: see information below.		
	Sales Tax: Californians please add 6.5% sales tax.		
		Total Amount	

Shipping and Handling: $3.50 for the first book and $1.00 for each additional book. Floppy disk add $1.50 for shipping and handling. Add $15.00 per book for overseas shipping and handling. If you have to have it NOW, we can ship product to you in 24 to 48 hours. For an additional $5.00 RUSH CHARGE for processing plus the actual cost of air freight, you'll be able to receive your item over night or in 2 days.

NO POSTAGE
NECESSARY
IF MAILED
IN THE
UNITED STATES

BUSINESS REPLY MAIL

FIRST CLASS PERMIT NO. 53 THOUSAND OAKS, CA

POSTAGE WILL BE PAID BY ADDRESSEE

New Riders Publishing
P.O. Box 4846
Thousand Oaks, CA 91359-9968